The Double Life of F

KINGSHUK NAG has been a journalist with *The Times of India* for the last sixteen years, and is currently the resident editor of its Hyderabad edition. He is a winner of the Prem Bhatia Award for outstanding political reporting for his coverage of the 2002 riots in Gujarat.

The Double Life of Ramalinga Raju

THE STORY OF INDIA'S BIGGEST CORPORATE FRAUD

KINGSHUK NAG

HarperCollins *Publishers* India
a joint venture with

New Delhi

First published in India in 2009 by
HarperCollins *Publishers* India
a joint venture with
The India Today Group

Copyright © Kingshuk Nag 2009

ISBN: 978-81-7223-908-4

2 4 6 8 10 9 7 5 3 1

Kingshuk Nag asserts the moral right to be identified
as the author of this book.

HarperCollins Publishers
A-53, Sector 57, NOIDA, Uttar Pradesh – 201301, India
77-85 Fulham Palace Road, London W6 8JB, United Kingdom
Hazelton Lanes, 55 Avenue Road, Suite 2900, Toronto, Ontario M5R 3L2
and 1995 Markham Road, Scarborough, Ontario M1B 5M8, Canada
25 Ryde Road, Pymble, Sydney, NSW 2073, Australia
31 View Road, Glenfield, Auckland 10, New Zealand
10 East 53rd Street, New York NY 10022, USA

Typeset in 10.5/15 Giovanni Book
Jojy Philip New Delhi 110 015

Printed and bound at
Thomson Press (India) Ltd.

For the thousands of investors who lost their
fortunes in India's biggest financial fraud

Contents

Acknowledgements

To a newsperson like me, who is used to writing copy of 600 to 700 words, the prospect of penning a book of 50,000 to 60,000 words has always been extremely daunting. However, when the Satyam scam broke, it presented a brilliant opportunity to bring out the story of Ramalinga Raju and Satyam in the form of a book. I was toying with this idea when Amit Agarwal, managing editor at HarperCollins India, called me and asked whether I would like to author a book on Satyam. It has been a delightful experience working with Amit and I would like to thank him for getting me into this project and for his editing of the book.

I must thank the dozens of persons connected to Satyam and the Rajus, who shared their insights with me and provided me with valuable information. While many of these sources do not want to be identified, they include serving and former executives of Satyam and some members of the erstwhile board of the company. I was also able to pick the brains of many top officials of Maytas. The Rajus' friends and business associates also gave me insights about their activities, as did government officials who had dealt with them.

Monotosh Sinha and Hekmumar, independent stock analysts based in Mumbai and Hyderabad respectively, explained to me the stock market aspects of Satyam and Maytas operations. To analyse the political angle, I met top politicians, including ministers of the Andhra Pradesh and central governments.

To corroborate and substantiate the information I got from these sources, I spent endless hours poring over documents pertaining to Satyam and Maytas, including not only their annual reports but also (in the case of Maytas) the red-herring prospectus filed during the time of the initial public offering (IPO). I also studied in detail the chargesheet filed by the CBI in the case and was privy to many details that are yet to be placed on record by the investigating agencies.

Getting Raju's side of the story was not easy but I was able to meet his son, Teja, who gave me the perspective from his father's side. I would also like to acknowledge the help I got from Raju's lawyer, Bharat Kumar, in this regard.

I have tried my best to be judicious to each character in the book, including Raju. The book is not a product of imagination. Where conversations have been recreated, I have tried to do so with reasonable verisimilitude, based on facts and information gathered by me. While the manuscript has been checked for factual errors, if any mistakes remain, they are mine alone.

Thanks are in place for my long-standing colleagues in *The Times of India*. Without their moral support this venture would not have got off the ground. I am thankful to the management of the company for posting me in Hyderabad. The book couldn't have been written but for that.

Finally, I would like to thank my wife, Swati, for bearing with my moods while I was writing the book!

Preface

In 1996, on a trip to Washington, I asked the chairman of the India Interest Group and senior executive at GE, Michael Gadbaw, what his take on liberalization in India was. His words still ring in my ears: 'India is an ancient country, a great country... It's a tiger waiting to be uncaged...an elephant ready to move... But why is it perpetually standing on the edge of greatness, why does this greatness never come?'

I think I have part of the answer now. This greatness never comes because of people like Ramalinga Raju, who subvert the march to progress and set the country back.

Although India has been a mixed economy since the beginning of the second five-year plan in 1956, the private sector really came into its own after the reforms process was initiated in 1991. These policies allowed entrepreneurs such as Azim Premji, N.R. Narayana Murthy and Sunil Mittal to unleash their creative zeal and build businesses that made the country proud. Ramalinga Raju also falls in this category of businessmen who made good their fortune post-1991.

Raju's story is remarkable in that he was a first-generation entrepreneur who started from scratch and built a $2-billion empire that cut across technology, realty and infrastructure sectors. And all this in a matter of a little over two decades, before he turned fifty-four. Little wonder then that Raju became an icon in his home town of Hyderabad, and a household name across India.

Somewhere down the line, as Raju was building his empire, his ambition got the better of him. He seemed to have lost his sense of right and wrong and his sense of balance, and began to think that the ends justified the means. Even after attending Harvard Business School, he did not foresee that he could not possibly go undetected forever for cooking up his balance sheets to the tune of thousands of crores of rupees.

Raju's story is also illustrative in the sense that it displays how a person exposed to the modern world could be propelled by feudal factors and carried away by tribal instincts. Raju lusted for land as if that was the only productive asset he had. For him the whole world revolved around his own immediate family and the Raju community.

The saga of Raju also exposes the close link between politics and business. Ramalinga Raju could not have become what he did without support first from Chandrababu Naidu (who put him on the dais with visiting US President Bill Clinton much to the chagrin of leading businessmen such as Rahul Bajaj) and then from Naidu's successor, the late Rajasekhara Reddy, whose government awarded him the metro rail project in Hyderabad. Raju was also smart enough to obtain the patronage of the former president of India, A.P.J. Abdul Kalam, whom he inducted on the board of his Emergency Medical Research Institute (EMRI).

The fact that Raju could carry on fudging the accounts of publicly listed company undetected for eight years reflects very poorly on corporate governance in the country. It raises questions about whether the independent directors on the boards of listed companies are merely sleeping directors content to collect their fees and perks. It brings up issues about auditors who vet the books of accounts of companies. How rigorously do they do their job? Are they truly above board? One also wonders about the effectiveness of our watchdog bodies.

Raju's crime – he allegedly siphoned off Satyam's money to finance his land deals and created fictitious revenues and profits in the company's books – has compromised the position of Indian corporates in a way that nobody has done before. Indian companies seeking to raise money from foreign bourses and willing to do business abroad will now find it a wee bit more difficult. Indian investors in India will also be a little more wary of putting their money in shares.

The only redeeming feature in the whole scenario is that Satyam was rehabilitated very quickly – within a span of four months – after Ramalinga Raju made that startling confession about cooking his revenues and profits on the morning of 7 January 2009.

One thing is clear, though – and this is not meant to be a justification of what Raju did. Raju would not have landed in this position if it hadn't been for the recessionary forces that hit the Indian shores by September 2008. Recession threw Raju off guard and closed all his options. In the end, he could do nothing but confess.

One of the most intriguing questions of the Raju saga is the reason for his confession. Why did he give himself up? With Raju behind bars and his lawyer refusing to carry my questions to him, the only option was to quiz Raju's elder son, Teja. Though never a part of Satyam, Teja said that his father fudged books and confessed to it only to save Satyam. Teja claimed that

Satyam was plagued by takeover threats and in order to stave off such threats, Raju created fictitious revenues and profits in the books of Satyam. And that he gave himself up because in the wake of the aborted merger of Satyam with Maytas Infra and Maytas Properties (the construction and real estate companies owned by Raju), the entire market was rife with rumours, which had the potential to destabilize Satyam and destroy it forever. 'My dad did everything that he did to save Satyam and the jobs of the 53,000 employees who worked there,' Teja said. It is a reasoning/justification that will not have many takers.

Granted that in the end Raju had no option but to confess, but why had he sold all his shares? Teja's explanation for this is a bit tenuous. He points out that his father was a first-generation entrepreneur, and though the family had business interests in agriculture, there was no one to tell him that it was not a wise move to start off with a promoters' equity holding of only 18 per cent (after the initial public issue in 1992, in which Raju offered 82 per cent to the public). This mistake was not repeated in the case of Maytas Infra, whose initial public issue was in 2007. The Raju family in this case held on to over 80 per cent of the equity. (However, Teja's claim turned out to be incorrect. It was found that just as in the case of Satyam, the Rajus had pledged most of their shares in Maytas Infra also to banks and financial institutions. The Company Law Board has now divested the Rajus of Maytas's control.)

Though corporate frauds are common in India and even in the developed world, the one committed by Raju is rare. In fact, there is only one other Satyam-like example in the corporate history of the world. This happened in the US in the mid-1930s, in a pharma company called McKesson & Robbins. In that instance, the chairman of the company, in league with four of his brothers who were also employed in the company, used to show huge export revenues, though there were no exports at all! Like Satyam, this company had fictitious ledgers, accounts books and false bills and it was listed on the New York Stock Exchange. Here the similarity ends. The McKesson fraud was discovered after the company's treasurer (equivalent of the chief financial officer of today) blew the whistle. When the police came to arrest the chairman, Philip Musica, he put a gun to his head and shot himself.

An interesting question relates to what is ultimately going to happen to Raju. Much will depend on how the US courts frame charges against him. If investigations by US agencies are able to nail Raju, he might go to jail for a couple of decades. The Indian legal system is not that robust and a resourceful man like Raju, even if convicted, will be in jail for a maximum of ten years. By common consent, once out of jail, he may have to spend his entire life fighting cases over the huge tracts of land that his family owns in Hyderabad. Indications are that many elements have already started grabbing land belonging to the Rajus. As for Raju's two sons, Teja and Rama Raju (junior), they probably have no future left in Hyderabad. In their home town, the sins of their father will always hang like an albatross around their necks. They may have a better future if they start life anew somewhere abroad.

Raju's is a gripping tale laced with greed, ambition and a father's love for his sons. It is a cautionary tale for our times.

Introduction: The Lust for Land

In his classic short story, 'How Much Land Does a Man Need?' Leo Tolstoy himself provides the answer to the question posed in the title: 'A man needs only six feet to cover the body from head to toe.'

The greed of the story's protagonist, Pakhom, for more land kills him in the end. Tolstoy wrote the story of a different land (Russia) at a different time (1880s) in a different context (feudal pre-revolution Russia). But the story of Ramalinga Raju, in essence, is not very different from that of Pakhom. Pakhom died and Raju is in jail because both were victims of their own avarice.

Raju's story is not merely about rapacious land acquisition – it is also about how he pawned his shareholding in Satyam as well as in his construction company, Maytas Infra, and how he allegedly siphoned off funds from both companies, to satisfy his craving. While the Russian peasant never broke the law, Raju thought nothing of doing so.

By the time he went behind bars, Raju, along with his family members, was officially the owner of 6,800 acres (9,000 acres, according to unofficial estimates) of prime land in Hyderabad,

Bangalore, Chennai and Nagpur, among other places. While most of it lay vacant, Raju was developing high-end commercial and housing spaces in some areas. It is difficult to put a value to this land, but Raju had on record estimated the value of his 6,800 acres at Rs 6,500 crore. By the same logic, 9,000 acres (the unofficial figure) would add up to more than Rs 8,500 crore. Even if one assumes that Raju had overestimated his land worth by 50 per cent, the value of his landholdings would be approximately Rs 4,000 crore.

Why Raju lusted for land is not clear, although it may have to do with his background and the milieu in which he was born and raised. Born in 1954, Raju grew up in the small hamlet of Bhimavaram in the West Godavari district of Andhra Pradesh. His father was a farmer who scouted for fortune around the state from the 1950s to the 1970s. Eventually, he was able to make money through farming and settled in Hyderabad, where he bought land, began grape cultivation, and called over relatives and extended family from back home to settle in an enclave set up by him. This enclave, in the outskirts of the city in those days, is quite within the present municipal limits of Hyderabad. Raju's relatives tell stories of how his father bought some of the best pieces of land in Hyderabad. This included a plot in the Bachupally area of Hyderabad, where Maytas Properties, a company set up in 2005 by the Rajus to foray into realty in a big way, started Maytas Hill County, an ambitious real estate development venture that involved high-end housing along with a special economic zone (SEZ).

It may not be out of place to point out that Ramalinga Raju hails from the Raju community, the equivalent of the Kshatriya caste of north India. Numerically very small – in total they do not account for more than four lakhs – the community is very closely knit. Many of them are related through marriage. The story goes that some five hundred years ago, the forefathers of the Rajus – who were possibly Rajputs from what is modern-day Rajasthan – came down through Orissa in search of fortune. Originally bearing weapons, they later took to land and became big farmers. Many of them have today diversified into land and real estate development. Land is an intrinsic part of their culture. One thing that may be noted, however, is that unlike many landowning groups, the Rajus have never been accused of being arrogant and overbearing.

Land reforms and redistribution policies were initiated by the Indian government in the 1950s, soon after the country attained independence. However, the experience of land reforms has been varied for different states. Andhra Pradesh is a good example of a state where land reforms have been conspicuous by their failure, though on paper over fifty-five lakh acres of land have been redistributed and it is illegal for any individual to possess more than fifty-four acres of land. The reality is that it is de facto possible for individuals to own hundreds and thousands of acres. The possibility of owning so much land obviously fuelled the ambitions of people so inclined, and Raju perhaps was one such person. Though Raju has been found out, he is not the only person to control such vast tracts of land in Andhra Pradesh. Large sections of the elite in the state own land to an extent that would be a near impossibility in most other states. It is in this milieu that Raju operated.

But if this was the environment in which Raju grew up, his world view was also shaped by his foreign stints. These stints helped him build an IT empire for which he got wide recognition. At the time of Raju's shock confession, Satyam was a software services company with revenues of more than $2 billion. With operations in sixty-six countries and over 500 clients, it was rated the fourth-largest IT company out of India.

There are three communities in India whose members can be found in large numbers in the US, UK, Canada and other parts of the developed world. The Gujaratis migrate abroad to set up small businesses and the Punjabis migrate in search of better opportunities. But the Telugu quest overseas is for education. Members of no other community in India go to the US in search of a degree – be it in science, technology, medicine or management – in so large a number as the Telugus do.

For the denizens of Andhra Pradesh this offshore search began in the mid-1970s, and one of the earliest birds to catch the worm was Raju, who went to the US for three different stints. The first was to acquire an MBA in the late 1970s, then to attend a course at Harvard Business School in the mid-1990s and again for a year to New York for business reasons in 2000–01. His stay in the US changed Raju's outlook only partially. He realized that the world was a global village and consciously decided to don the mindset of a virtual immigrant. Thus, even while staying in India, Raju behaved like a global citizen. But he was unable to do away with his deeply ingrained feudal mindset. This led to contradictions: on the one hand he was running a global IT company, and on the other he was acting like a feudal lord whose primary interest was acquisition of land.

It is quite clear that Raju used all his wealth – generated from the IT company – to buy real estate. Before 1999, land purchases by Raju were funded from dividends earned from Satyam and other incomes of the family. But with Hyderabad beginning to grow fast and becoming a global name in the IT industry, Raju stepped up his land purchases. In need of more funds, he began selling off his shares and that of his family members in Satyam. Being a closely knit family, selling off shares of his close relations did not pose much of a problem. Since the land laws in Andhra Pradesh did not allow any individual to own more than fifty-four acres, Raju began spawning privately held companies to purchase land. By the time the law caught up with him, Raju had set up over 325 companies, which were, on paper, owned by his immediate and extended family. The companies were duly registered and stated their official purpose to be agricultural and allied pursuits. All of them had their official address at only a dozen-odd locations in Hyderabad city.

By 2006, Raju was buying land so furiously that sale of his Satyam shares could no longer match his hunger for land. So, instead of selling the shares he pledged the shares to financial institutions as collateral and raised money. Raju may have begun purchasing land following the family tradition, but he was not interested in making money from its cultivation and being a gentleman farmer. Instead he wanted to add value to the land by getting into the business of realty. From here, a small hop, step and jump took him to the domain of construction and infrastructure development.

Another interesting aspect of Raju's story is that like Dhritarashtra in the Mahabharata, Raju was blinded by his love for his two sons, Teja and Rama Jr. Both were educated in the US, and were inducted into business in early 2001 and 2005, respectively. Raju could go to any extent to promote their interests. In the last few years, much to the detriment of Satyam, he focussed on the two companies he was building for his sons – Maytas Infra, promoted by Teja, and Maytas Properties, promoted by Rama Jr. In his quest to promote his sons, he also sidelined his youngest brother Rama Raju (managing director at Satyam and popularly known as Ramu), who was like Lakshmana of the Ramayana to him.

Rama Raju often articulated Raju's views to the world and acted as his interlocutor. Before 2005, he looked after the real estate and construction business of the family, but Raju pushed him out of this activity to prop up his sons. This led to some tension in the family, but brought up in a culture where elders are respected and obeyed, Rama did not go public with his grouse or even make an issue out of it. Raju himself showed the same respect to his father, Satyanarayana, who greatly influenced him. In fact, the name Satyam is a short form of Satyanarayana. Raju also had another brother, Suryanarayana, who was associated with Maytas. Said to be an intermediate college dropout, Raju used him extensively for his land dealings.

In some senses, Raju was extremely lucky, at least to start with. He was a chance IT entrepreneur. Raju co-founded Satyam in 1987 along with a distant cousin, D.V.S. Raju, largely at the instance of the latter. While Raju was a commerce graduate and MBA, D.V.S. Raju was a techie and had done a BE and MTech. Within a few years, the company became a roaring success, as it pioneered the concept of offshoring (preparing software for overseas clients) that subsequently developed into a very big industry in India.

But Raju would have been a big IT industry man and nothing more if fate had not intervened in the form of Chandrababu Naidu. Determined to make a name as India's most modern chief minister, Naidu sought to showcase Hyderabad as a shining symbol of an emerging India that could dare to take on the developed world. In his endeavour, Naidu sought to use the software industry to project Hyderabad. That's where Raju's utility to Naidu came in. Naidu was so impressed by Raju that he presented him to the world as the icon of the new Hyderabad and chose the occasion of the visit of the then US president, Bill Clinton, to do so.

Raju was smart in capitalizing on his new-found status to further his land purchasing business. Land was an investment for him – he bought it to speculate or to develop real estate on it. Raju was helped by the fact that as the city grew rapidly, so did land prices, but no profits from his land dealings came to Satyam – it is believed that the money went into buying more land. Raju also used his proximity to the powers that be to shield himself from law when he was questioned about income tax irregularities in 2002.

It must be pointed out that Raju was never squeaky clean in business affairs. A good example is a loan of Rs 50 lakh he took from an Andhra Pradesh government agency in the early 1980s to start a spinning mill. Raju never returned the principal or paid interest on the loan.

Raju's questionable means started surfacing at the turn of the century when his Satyam Infoway (an internet service provider that is no longer part of the Satyam stable) bought a clutch of websites overseas for an exorbitant price. That is when allegations first started flying that the entire amount did not go to the seller, that a part of it could have come back to Raju. Nothing was proven. Satyam Infoway had been listed on the Nasdaq, the American stock exchange for technology shares, and was therefore cash rich. Satyam was also one of the infamous K-10 shares that bull operator Ketan Parekh, who was subsequently put behind bars for rigging the market, was speculating in in 2000-02. Raju's entanglement with Ketan Parekh and whether Raju was also party to jacking up the price of his own shares by misusing inside information is still being investigated. Also being investigated is whether some of the proceeds from the public issue of Satyam Infoway on Nasdaq and Satyam on the New York Stock Exchange (NYSE) were swindled.

Raju started cheating his Satyam shareholders at the beginning of 2001. By his own admission, this is when he started fudging his book of accounts by showing higher than actual revenues and profits for Satyam to make the company look impressive and boost its share prices. As the years progressed, Raju was emboldened by the fact that he was not found out. This propelled him to fudge more, and the process reached its climax in 2008, when Raju began to manufacture figures at will, as a result of which Satyam became a $2 billion company. If Raju had been around, Satyam would have shown revenues of $2.3 billion for the financial year 2008-09, say those who are in the know of things.

Other than manipulating figures of Satyam's revenues and profits, Raju is also thought to have salted away part of the company's export proceeds. The suspected modus operandi was to channelize the payments received from clients overseas through fictitious (benami) accounts. However, this is not yet proven, and Raju has stoutly denied having ever done this. The CBI, which is investigating all export proceeds of Satyam and also the money it raised through its public issue abroad, has zeroed in on some suspect accounts to which this money was transferred. These accounts stand in the name of US nationals and the CBI has now sought the help of Interpol to proceed further in the matter. The CBI suspects that there are more such accounts. Simultaneously, the Enforcement Directorate is also looking for evidence of similar transgressions.

Spiralling stock prices of Satyam not only raised the rating of the company in the market, they also directly benefitted Raju because he was selling his own shares in Satyam. The money was, of course, being used to buy more land and promote his construction and infrastructure company.

One reason the BJP lost the 2004 general elections was its 'Shining India' card. But due to the world economic environment, India did actually start shining 2005 onwards. Raju realized this and began to fully capitalize on the new situation. He got into infrastructure development in a big way and worked assiduously to fill the order books of the two Maytas companies. To promote these companies he began to dip into the resources of Satyam more than ever before, even as rumours of him selling his IT company to IBM started surfacing at periodic intervals.

Without realizing it, Raju was shutting himself off from Satyam, the company that actually made him what he was. He was either selling his shares in the company or pledging them to raise loans to buy more land (while there is no bar on pledging, post-Raju, the SEBI has stipulated that promoters of companies doing this have to mandatorily inform the bourses). However, Raju's confession claims that the money was being raised to be pumped into Satyam.

This went on till 2008, when fate caught up with him. Trouble came from unexpected quarters and was not specific to him. With a slowdown setting in, the value of Raju's assets in land started diminishing as the real estate sector went downhill. Financial institutions from whom Raju had borrowed money bayed for his blood because he had kept his shares with them as collateral (while his stake in Satyam was 100 per cent to begin with, it became about 18 per cent after the first public issue, and almost 0 per cent at the end).

With share prices falling and the worth of the collateral declining, the banks wanted to be compensated. Raju, of course, did not have the cash to do so, his wealth having declined greatly. However, even in his hour of crisis, Raju was indulging in brinkmanship. His greed and ambition had still not deserted him.

The events that led to Raju's confession began in August 2008, when Maytas Infra won the project to implement the Rs 12,500-crore Hyderabad metro rail system. What was surprising was not that Maytas won the contract but what it offered as the price for getting it. All over the world, metro rail systems are not viable without government subsidy. In India, such projects are sought to be made viable by the grant of central government funds called Viability Gap Funding or VGF. But Ramalinga Raju amazed everybody by declaring that he did not want any VGF. On the contrary, he undertook to pay the government a hefty licence fee. Although the project promoter was to be given a considerable amount of land for commercial development to help make the project viable, Raju's promise to pay money to the government immediately led to suspicion that he was viewing the rail project as a real estate venture. There were also allegations that Raju was hand in glove with top politicians to have bid for the project in this unrealistic manner. It was suggested that this outlandish bidding was suggested to him by an important person in government. But nothing is proven.

Raju took on this massive rail project just as the global recession hit Indian shores. That made it an even more foolhardy decision. Raju was standing on the brink of disaster but still did not realize it. His gameplan was to make his money through property development. He planned to petition the government to extend the length of the railway route. But before doing so, he planned to buy land around the extended portion. He also aimed to get the route extended to areas where he already owned land.

When the hour of reckoning came close, Raju sought to raise money from the market using his personal goodwill. But nobody was there to help him – the market was dry and all the liquidity in the system had been sucked out. In the end, Raju conjured up the plan to merge Maytas with Satyam and rammed the proposal past his board of directors on 16 December 2008.

Ostensibly the merger was to offer a diversification avenue for Satyam, which was hit by the IT slowdown. But Raju's strategy was to cover up the missing cash of Satyam with the real assets of Maytas. The transfer of payment from Satyam to Maytas to acquire the latter would be only on paper. The coffers of Satyam were empty but then who would complain? Eighty-five per cent of the shares of Maytas were held by Raju's family members, who presumably would not object to anything.

However, by now luck had deserted Raju and fate was catching up with him. Investors and analysts at the bourses, sensing foul play, violently rejected the idea. But they did not see through Raju's game. They perceived that Raju was trying to palm off a not-too-well-performing Maytas to Satyam. Actually Raju was doing the reverse: he was trying to save Satyam by using Maytas. It may be worth noting that Raju's troubles came from the US. Had his shares been listed only on the Indian bourses there would have been nothing for him to fear. He could have managed public opinion in the country well. But the analysts and investors, mostly FIIs, were all from the US, and they were not in a mood to take any unacceptable behaviour from a company promoter. If the US connection did him in, it was also an association that had catapulted Raju to the big league of software exporters and enabled him to raise millions of dollars from the bourses.

One of the most mysterious angles of the Satyam case is Raju's confession. Granted that he was involved in wrongdoing, but what was the need for Raju to confess? He could have gone along as if nothing had happened and waited for the law to catch up with him. Was it that Raju could not bear the tension any more? We have no way of knowing, though it is reasonably certain that it was not a conscience call. Most likely, it was a damage limitation exercise – by doing so he would at least get the sympathy of some who would be taken in by his admission of guilt.

It is clear that Raju confessed when he realized that he had been found out. Satyam had hired Merrill Lynch to look into strategic options after its failed attempt to merge with Maytas. It took Merrill Lynch just about a week to figure out that the books of Satyam were cooked. On 6 January 2009, just a day before Raju's confession, Merrill Lynch wrote to Raju that they had found material irregularities in Satyam's accounts, and what is worse, marked a copy of the letter to the SEBI. Realizing that the game was up, Raju wrote a confession letter admitting to his wrongdoing and resigned before the market regulator made it public.

But even if the Merrill Lynch letter became public, where was the need for him to quit Satyam? In all likelihood this was because Raju realized that he hardly had any shares left in the company. All the Satyam shares that he had pawned had been sold off in the open market by financial institutions. Although Raju was still the promoter of the company, he figured that without shares he was defenceless and could be voted out in his own company.

There is another reason for the confession: he wanted to protect Maytas at all costs. Raju realized, even in his hour of crisis, that the longer he hung on to Satyam the more the chances that mud being thrown at him would stick to Maytas. Raju figured that he would be able to reconcile with the loss of Satyam, but not that of Maytas, the company that he was building for his sons.

But that was not to be. On 31 August 2009, Raju was dealt a second major blow. The Company Law Board (CLB) ordered that the Rajus be divested of their control of Maytas Infra and that the company be given to the Infrastructure Leasing and Financial Services Ltd (IL & FS), a consortium of banks which had shown an interest in acquiring it. The order came after the central government, realizing that the stakes of the Rajus in Maytas Infra (as had happened in the case of Satyam earlier) had effectively fallen to very low levels, approached the CLB for 'directions' on how to deal with the company. In an irony of sorts,

Teja Raju (for whom Raju had built Maytas) was also ordered to resign from the company's board. The stake of the Rajus, which was as high as 84 per cent in October 2007, effectively fell to zero with this order.

In an encore of the Satyam story, the Rajus had been pawning their shares in Maytas Infra too. The mortgaging of Maytas shares began shortly after the company raised money through its public issue less than two years ago. When the Rajus were kicked out of Maytas, they had mortagaged 62 per cent of their stake in the company and had borrowed money from banks and financial institutions. That left the Rajus with 22 per cent shares in Maytas, but this would be 'locked in' as per SEBI regulations till October 2010. These regulations stipulate that promoters of companies cannot sell or mortage a certain part of their shares for three years after its public issue. While passing the order for changing the managment of Maytas, the CLB also noted that the company was passing through a liquidity crunch so severe that the operations of the company had virtually come to a standstill. The exit of the Rajus from Maytas followed the declaration of annual results for Maytas Infra for 2008-09, which showed a staggering loss of Rs 490 crore.

One question that may be asked is: how is it that Raju was never found out all these years? After all, Satyam's equity was listed on both Indian and American bourses, before whom significant disclosures have to be made. The answer is to be found in the poor quality of corporate governance in India. Satyam's board was studded with stars: a professor from the Harvard Business School, the director of the Indian School of Business, a former cabinet secretary to the Government of India, and one of the developers of Pentium. How could this high-profile board not smell a rat?

Most of the members were sleeping directors content with being on the board of Satyam. They had other preoccupations and served on the boards of many other companies. Above all, they had an unshakeable faith in Raju and were taken in by his soft-spoken nature and modesty. At least one of them, Krishna Palepu from the Harvard Business School, was a non-executive, part-time director who was being paid a significant amount of money for consultancy work doled out by Satyam. He had earlier served on the board of a US subsidiary of Satyam called Value Compass. That company failed. Several directors on the nine-member board (including the two Raju brothers and a whole-time director on the rolls of Satyam) hailed from Andhra Pradesh and saw the company as Andhra's pride. One of the directors was a Raju. They had no reasons to suspect foul play in the company.

Another crucial reason for Raju not being detected is the fact that the company's auditors, Subramani Gopalakrishnan and Srinivas Talluri of PricewaterhouseCoopers, were possibly in league with him. Their guilt remains to be proven in a court of law but in what seems to be a manifestation of gross misconduct, they signed the balance sheets of Satyam knowing fully well that the figures indicated in the books were false, it is being said. What is more, they actively participated in the fraud by indulging in pretences. Auditors are expected to write to banks and independently confirm balances reported by companies. However, Satyam's auditors pretended to send letters to banks, leaving copies in Satyam's computers, but actually did not send them, say investigators. In the few cases they did, when the banks presented a different picture, the auditors swept the findings under the carpet. It is believed that the auditors were doing all this without the knowledge of the management of Pricewaterhouse.

So deeply were the auditors involved in aiding Raju that when a whistle-blower (an insider who used an alias and has still not been identified) reported at the end of December 2008 that the accounts of Satyam were fudged, they declared that the whistle-blower's contention was false.

Raju also succeeded because he was able to get some unscrupulous employees to do his bidding. Mediocre characters, elevated to high positions undeservedly, they were mesmerized by Raju and were additionally silenced by the grant of employee stock options.

Good public relations was the key to Raju's success. In spite of being introverted and shy, Raju had built goodwill and contacts (including through dubious means) at all relevant places. He knew the Federation of Indian Chambers of Commerce and Industry (FICCI) bosses closely and was part of the Confederation of Indian Industry crowd, regularly seen at their dos in Delhi and Mumbai. Raju had solid contacts at the government level, had basked in the glory of Chandrababu Naidu (whose influence extended to the national level), and then assiduously cultivated Naidu's successor, the late Rajasekhara Reddy.

Part of Raju's goodwill also emanated from the fact that he was (seemingly) engaged in corporate social work on a massive scale. His Emergency Management and Research Institute (EMRI) pioneered in India the concept of an emergency number 108, which could be called to activate an ambulance service in times of need. Though the scheme was run with government money in Andhra Pradesh, Gujarat, Rajasthan and other states, Raju controlled the EMRI and the show. There was significant rub-off in terms of goodwill from EMRI as also from the Byrraju Foundation set up by Raju for social work. In fact, FICCI gave him an award for the best corporate social responsibility (CSR).

EMRI had a high-profile board that included former Indian president A.P.J. Abdul Kalam, but unknown to the board, corporate governance in the organization was as bad as in Satyam.

This never became public but post Raju, when suitors seeking to take over the organization did a due diligence report, they found questionable practices, such as improper documentation of assets, purchases, etc.

Raju's exemplary behaviour – he never raised his voice even when provoked to the extreme – also conveyed a positive impression on whoever came in contact with him. He was a liberal man and could not say no to anyone. This added to his aura. His clannish mindset meant that he cared for his people. They continually spread the good word about him and this resulted in a larger-than-life image for Raju and Satyam, specially in Hyderabad. This rubbed off on employees as well. Not only were they treated with admiration in Hyderabad, they were also given discounts in many restaurants and hotels. Even grocers' shops would give them special discounts and they were much sought after for matrimonial alliances.

Above all, one of the most important reasons why Raju was not discovered lay in his genius of running his empire in a very compartmentalized way. It was somewhat like how a mafia operates or the intelligence department works. In Satyam, no manager knew – beyond the very basics – what the other manager was doing.

The finance and human resources departments in particular, which handled the most sensitive information and where the maximum amount of fudging took place, were kept under wraps. Nobody in Satyam, including the top managers, had a clue about the functioning of the finance department. There were also watertight compartments between Satyam and Maytas, and between Satyam and EMRI and the Byrraju Foundation. 'Once, a junior manager of Satyam was sent off to Byrraju Foundation for two months. When Raju chanced upon this fact he was furious and ordered the man back,' a senior Satyam manager recalls.

While confessing, Raju had mentioned the senior leadership of Satyam by name and said that they were not aware of the goings-on. Yet, there are some doubts. In spite of the tight compartments, it is possible that some of the top managers of Satyam did know what has happening but kept mum. Perhaps they were not aware of the entire picture, but certainly would have had some inkling of it. Some of them were possibly collaborators, but with the law closing in, they are now feigning ignorance.

Although he requisitioned the services of his extended family for his various activities, Raju followed a policy of sharing information with them on a strict need-to-know basis. He was not at all forthcoming with them. As Raju was so successful, they were in awe of him and did not ask any questions. Raju told them specifically to be discreet. He also kept his immediate family out of the loop on most matters.

Ramalinga Raju is not the only financial fraudster to be exposed in India. Every ten years or so, a major financial scandal breaks in the country. But in the sheer audacity and nature of the fraud, Raju outdid the earlier scams of Harshad Mehta and Ketan Parekh. The scale of Raju's con is large by Indian standards, but perhaps not so by global reckoning. This, of course, does not absolve Raju of the crime he committed.

Barely a month before Raju gave in, on 10 December 2008, a New York resident and former non-executive chairman of Nasdaq, Bernard Lawrence Madoff, revealed that he had been running a giant asset management fraud, called the Ponzi scheme, named after a notorious scamster who pioneered the concept in the US a hundred years ago. Essentially, Madoff's modus operandi – like anybody else's operating in the business – was to take in money from investors and pay returns to them. The returns were not extraordinarily high at 10 per cent, but Madoff paid even when the economy was doing badly. However, Madoff was not paying the returns based on his earnings out of the deposits. Rather, he was paying the first depositor out of the deposits made by the second depositor, and the second depositor out of the deposits made by the third depositor, and so on.

Madoff, like Raju who came after him, gave in when he realized that he could not carry on the game any further. Billed as the largest investor fraud ever committed by a single person, the Madoff scam is estimated to be worth $65 billion. In comparison, the Raju scam was worth only Rs 7,500 crore, or a little over $1.5 billion.

Six months after he shocked the world with his confession, Ramalinga Raju sits in jail waiting for bail and a fast trial. Keeping him company in Chanchalguda jail in Hyderabad is brother Rama Raju and CFO Srinivasa Vadlamani. All three of them, who conspired to cheat lakhs of investors, share the same cell in the high-security jail. Raju has plenty of time to look back on his life.

ONE

The Confession

It was the moment of reckoning. Ramalinga Raju knew he had been found out. DSP Merrill Lynch, the firm Raju had hired on 27 December 2008 to look into strategic options after Satyam's failed attempt to merge with Maytas and to recommend ways to strengthen corporate governance in Satyam, had blown the whistle on Satyam's accounts. The best course for him was to own up to his fraud before the world woke up to the contents of Merrill Lynch's letter to him, in which the firm had said that it was unable to continue with its assignment because it had found 'material accounting irregularities' in the books of the company. It had not elaborated what it meant by the term 'material irregularities', but the investment and analyst community understood very well the implication: Satyam's balance sheet was fudged.

DSP Merrill Lynch had been given only ten days to produce a report, which was to be presented before the company's board at its next meeting on 10 January 2009. The appointment of Merrill Lynch had been sparked off by the growing investor unrest about the way in which the fourth-largest Indian IT company was being run. Investors had been alleging since 16 December – when Ramalinga Raju had proposed the merger of Satyam and Maytas – that the Rajus were running Satyam, a publicly owned company, as their personal jagir.

Raju had no defence. Of course, Merrill Lynch had not been able to figure out the extent of the irregularities, but there would now be increased pressure for a special audit to check Satyam's books. To make things worse for Raju, Merrill Lynch had marked a copy of their letter to the corporate watchdog SEBI and to the Bombay Stock Exchange (BSE). These two organizations were bound to make the revelations public.

The boy from Bhimavaram realized that his time was up. He took an instant decision to quit the company that he had built from scratch over the last twenty-one years. 'Tomorrow morning I will write to our board of directors and also the stock exchanges, informing them of my resignation,' Raju decided. It was the evening of 6 January 2009.

Raju picked up the phone and called his son Teja, who was quite unaware of the goings-on at Satyam. 'There could be some trouble with law enforcement agencies. Be a little careful. Keep away from home tomorrow if possible,' Raju said. But he made no mention of the fact that he would make a confessional statement the next morning. Teja was confused but thought that his father probably anticipated an income tax raid.

Raju then called up his lawyer, Bharat Kumar, and asked him to come over. 'Bharat garu, I want to resign from Satyam tomorrow morning. I will write a letter to the board of directors to this effect,' Raju told the lawyer. The lawyer, who had been helping Raju with his cases for the last two years, was shocked. 'Don't do that, Sir. Where is the need for this?' he pleaded. But Raju was firm.

Interestingly, Raju did not call his wife, Nandini, and tell her of his plans. Nandini was not part of Satyam's executive team but she would not have been surprised to hear the bad news. Raju had been tense for the last three weeks, and more so since the New Year. Though he never discussed business at home, Raju had told her that the family holding in Satyam had now touched rock bottom. On 1 January, it was less than 2 per cent. In another few weeks, the Rajus were likely to be left shareless in their own company.

Before talking to his son, Teja, Raju had already contacted his brother, Rama Raju, who was also the managing director of Satyam, and told him that both of them would have to exit from the company. Rama had been Raju's shadow for the last thirty years and knew everything that was happening in Satyam. There was no need to explain anything to him.

Early next morning, Raju called his father-in-law, D.S. Raju. The old man was surprised as Raju hardly ever called him. What the retired engineer, who had spent part of his working life in Germany, heard, put him in a tizzy. A little later his daughter, Nandini, also called him to say there was no reason for him to worry. 'You know your son-in-law is not the person to do anything wrong. I myself came to know only yesterday,' Nandini said.

It was 7 January 2009 – the day of Vaikunth Ekadasi. For the god-fearing Telugus, this is one of the holiest days in the year, when all the gods, led by Lord Vishnu, are believed to descend from heaven to earth. People go to temples to pray on this day and take a dip in holy rivers.

Though Raju had decided to quit Satyam on the evening of 6 January, a couple of days earlier he had shared with his community seniors that life was becoming tough for him. At a community meeting, he had also expressed apprehensions that he could get into a legal tangle. The meeting had, needless to say, convened at Raju's instance. The venue of the meeting was Satyam Enclave in Medchal in Greater Hyderabad, where there is a settlement of the prosperous amongst the Rajus. In the past, the Rajus were rulers of small principalities in coastal Andhra Pradesh, but today they are mainly into business, especially real estate. The settlement in Medchal had been established by Ramalinga's father, Satyanarayana. Most of those who live here are related to Raju by blood and many others by marriage.

Raju did not mince any words and came straight to the point. He said that the books of Satyam were not in order and that the company did not have much cash in its coffers. In view of this, he was mulling the option of quitting the company. 'I wonder if there is anything else I can do. Maybe this is the only way in which Satyam can be saved. But I could run into problems with the law,' Raju said.

There was palpable tension in the room. 'Don't be crazy. Why do you have to make an announcement on your own that Satyam does not have any cash?' said one of those present. 'If you are caught, you are caught. Till that time you don't have to stand up and tell the whole world about your predicament,' said someone else. 'Don't commit harakiri,' proffered another. The discussion went on for some time. But Raju insisted that he would consider the option of resigning, his resolve showing no signs of weakening.

There was silence in the room; everybody knew that Ramalinga would listen to no one and that it was useless to try and persuade him to think otherwise. As the conversation resumed, someone pointed out that it would be better if Ramalinga gave himself up in India, as the law here was more lenient. But with Satyam being listed on the New York Stock Exchange, there was a possibility that a case could be filed in the US courts. That would be disastrous, because an Indian would not find the US legal system so easy to negotiate. And the US courts were known to hand out long sentences. Raju could land up with a sentence of a hundred years. This argument clinched the issue. All agreed that Raju could quit Satyam if he so desired. They also resolved to contribute funds to finance his legal battle. 'We are with you. Don't worry. We will fight for you. Things will soon become normal. You have done so much for the community, this is the least that we owe you,' said a family elder as the meeting came to an end.

After talking to Rama and Teja post his decision to resign on the evening of 6 January, Raju called a trusted manager to his office. This executive was one of the high fliers in the company and was known to have a good command over English. Raju explained to him the reason for calling him. 'I have drafted a letter addressed to our board of directors. I want you to go through it and polish it.' Then, without waiting for an answer, Raju went ahead to explain what he sought to communicate, and passed on a note that his lawyer had earlier given him, which in essence explained the problems in Satyam.

It was this letter, redrafted by his executive, which Raju dispatched to the stock exchange as soon as it opened for trade the next morning, on Vaikunth Ekadasi. A copy of the letter was marked to the chairman of SEBI as well. The fifty-four-year-old IT czar, who over the last few years had become an iconic figure, confessed that his situation was like 'riding a tiger and not knowing how to get off without being eaten'.

Raju wrote that the cash and bank balances of his company as reflected in the previous quarterly results of 30 September 2008 were inflated. 'For the September quarter (Q2) we reported a revenue of Rs 2,700 crores and an operating margin of Rs 649 crores (24 per cent of revenues) as against the actual revenues of

Rs 2,112 crores and an actual operating margin of Rs 61 crores (3 per cent of revenues). This has resulted in artificial cash and bank balances going up by Rs 588 crore in Q2 alone.'

Raju also wrote that he had been inflating the profits for the last several years. 'What started as a marginal gap between the actual operating profit and the one reflected in the books of account continued to grow over the years. It attained unmanageable proportions as the size of the company operations grew significantly... The differential in the real profits and the one reflected in the books was further accentuated by the fact that the company had to carry additional resources and assets to justify higher level of operations – thereby significantly increasing the costs,' Raju wrote.

The letter ran into five pages and ended saying: 'I am now prepared to subject myself to the laws of the land and face consequences thereof.' He also explained in the letter that the merger of Satyam and Maytas was precisely to bring cash to Satyam. Raju also said that he had pledged his shares in Satyam to raise funds to the tune of Rs 1,230 crore to be invested in the company. This was to make up for the cash that Satyam never had but was shown in the books. Raju also asserted that no shares had ever been sold by him for personal gain. He stated that the last straw was the selling off of the pledged shares by financial institutions because of 'margin triggers' (in lay terms, pressure from the banks to make up for the loss of value of their collateral – in this case, shares of Satyam).

Pointing out that he had promoted the company for the last twenty years, during which Satyam had grown to a 53,000-strong company with a presence in sixty-six countries, Ramalinga Raju also gave a clean chit to senior executives of Satyam, saying they were not party to any wrongdoing in the company. Raju also absolved his immediate and extended family members and those of his brother, Rama Raju. Rama Raju was not explicitly referred to in the letter, but the way it was drafted made it clear that he was complicit in the fraud. Satyam's chief financial officer, Srinivasa Vadlamani, was also not in the list of executives given a clean chit by Raju.

While tendering his resignation, Raju also took some decisions on how Satyam would go forward: he named Ram Mynampati, the only full-time director on the board of the company, as the interim chief executive officer (CEO). Appealing to the board to hold together in this 'crucial time', Raju recommended a 'restatement of accounts' of the company and suggested that board member T.R. Prasad (former cabinet secretary to the Government of India) was the right person to mobilize support for the company from the government. In the end, Raju 'sincerely apologized' to his employees and hoped that in this hour of crisis, they would stand by the company.

Before sending off the letter, Raju called up business associates with whom he dealt on a daily basis and briefed them on the gist of what he was about to confess. One of them was Venkat Chengavalli, executive director of EMRI. 'We have spoken every morning for the last one and a half years. But you will not hear from me any more,' Ramalinga told Chengavalli. 'I am resigning from the board of Satyam and also that of EMRI,' Raju said as he hung up. Chengavalli was stunned. He could not reconcile himself to the fact that this soft-spoken person, who spoke to him daily without fail, was a master fraud.

Sumant Nath (name changed) was at his desk in Satyam's corporate headquarters in Hi Tech City in Hyderabad when he heard about Raju's confession. An IIM graduate and a vice-president in the corporate strategy group of the company, Nath had been feeling disturbed for a few days. As a senior member of the strategy group, he had prior knowledge of the diversification plans of the company. But when Raju called for a board meeting on 16 December and proposed a merger of Satyam and Maytas, he was stunned because he was never part of any discussion on this matter. Questions came to his mind as he tried to convince himself that the proposal must have been mooted for the good of the company.

Nath had seen Raju closely for the last two years and had grown fond of him. He respected Raju for his depth of analysis and remembered that he had predicted at least a year ago that there would be a slowdown in the Indian economy because the subprime crisis in the US would go out of hand. This was a time when everybody was gung ho about the economy.

When Nath downloaded a copy of Raju's confession from the website of the stock exchange, he realized that his god had feet of clay. But the forty-five-year-old executive was more shocked to learn that the operating margin of Satyam was just 3 per cent and not 24 per cent as he believed. He wondered how that could be true. All top IT companies like Infosys, Tata Consultancy Services and Wipro had similar operating margins (almost 20 to 22 per cent). Satyam was almost in the same league as these three giants. Was Satyam so inefficient and its costs so high that the operating margin and profits had taken a nosedive, Nath asked himself. A person in Satyam was as competent as a techie working in Wipro or Infosys, he thought. Then why was Satyam's performance so poor? He had no answers.

Monotosh Sinha, a senior analyst and executive director of a leading investment firm, had just arrived in his office that morning when news of Raju's letter reached him. For a moment Sinha was stunned, but then he had had his suspicions about the state of Satyam's affairs. Sinha was tracking the Satyam story closely for his company and over the last few days, he had pored over many documents and read the Satyam balance sheet closely. He was sceptical when the company reported a staggering Rs 1,700 crore in its current account. Only a fool would keep that kind of money in a non-interest-paying account. Did the money exist at all? The analyst had thought that the truth would be out on 17 January, when Satyam would announce its Q3 (third quarter) results. With the company in the limelight, the auditors would go an extra mile to check whether the cash reported existed in the bank accounts of the company at all. If the cash was non-existent, the auditors would blow the whistle. But it was 7 January and Raju had confessed.

Sinha knew that he had been on the right track. But almost immediately another question came to his mind. Why had Raju confessed? Was he looking for public sympathy in his native Andhra Pradesh, where he was an icon? Did he know that his game was up and therefore wanted to wash his sins? Was Raju playing a game? Was he confessing to a lesser crime than what he had committed? Had he actually pilfered a huge sum of money, running into hundreds of crores, over the last five years and was now trying to put the lid on the can of worms by claiming that he had merely cooked his balance sheet? Sinha had no answers, but he knew that the punishment for falsifying figures would be less severe than swindling hundreds of crores from a listed company that had thousands of shareholders.

When Sumant Nath stepped out of his cabin, there was pandemonium in the Satyam office premises. Some of the staff had become hysterical – they did not know whether they still had their jobs or whether Satyam would continue to exist. Some did not fear that the company would close shop, but were not sure whether they would get their salary cheque at the end of the month. Other employees were switching on the television to find out how the world was reacting. Yet others were being practical – they began taking out copies of their curriculum vitae. By the end of the day, approximately 6,000 resumes of Satyamites had been uploaded on the site of a leading job portal.

Nath's head began to reel. He felt cheated and betrayed – the brand that he had boasted of and was proud to be associated with was based on falsehoods. His mind went to the numerous mails circulated by the Satyam management over the last fortnight assuring them that everything was fine. He also wondered how the top management knew nothing of the matter. Ram Mynampati was a whole-time director on the board of Satyam; he also controlled 60 per cent of the company's business. How was it possible that Myanampati did not know anything? A sense of having been fooled overcame him. Such thoughts were crossing his mind when he came to know that droves of TV crews had assembled below. The security guards were sensible enough to shut the gates. Only a small side gate was kept open. Then somebody said that at least the women employees should be allowed to go home. Those wearing salwar kameez covered their faces with their dupattas as they left the building. They were understandably traumatized and did not want to be captured on camera in their state of shock and distress.

With news spreading that Raju had cheated Satyam shareholders, the police got on the job. They feared that frustrated shareholders in their anger could attack Satyam establishments. Immediately, security was stepped up outside Satyam offices. A security net was also cast around Raju's house in Jubilee Hills.

Six hundred kilometers away, in Mumbai, there was a bloodbath on Dalal Street. Anybody and everybody who had shares of Satyam scrambled to offload the scrip. The share plunged. So great was the impact of Raju's revelations that it shook the very foundations of the Bombay Stock Exchange. The market collapsed, and by the end of trading hours at 3 p.m., the BSE Sensex had lost 749 points and wiped off $23 billion worth of investors' wealth. Satyam's stock, which had closed at Rs 179 (for an equity share of par value of Rs 2), fell off the cliff and ended at Rs 40.

Many pensioners and other investors, who had put their entire savings in the company's scrip, had become penniless. A schoolteacher in Phagwara, Punjab, could not bear the shock and took his life. Some others had to be rushed to hospitals. Institutional investors, who had put in money belonging to individuals looking for returns, also lost huge sums. The Life Insurance Corporation of India lost a whopping Rs 949 crore.

But such is the way of the world that even as there was a bloodbath, speculators were wondering how to make money in the situation. They wanted to buy Satyam shares in the hope that this free fall would be arrested and that prices would go up in a day or two. However, they were outnumbered by those who wanted to exit the Satyam scrip.

The shares would have crashed on the New York Stock Exchange too. Here, Satyam's American Depository Receipt (ADR) was listed and quoted at $9.35 at the end of the previous day's trade. But the bourse managers did not want to take a risk and suspended trade indefinitely on the Satyam ADR. Investors lost their money in the now dud Satyam equity, but Raju and his immediate family remained unaffected. He had lost his shares before the rest of the world had pressed the panic button. There would be no further loss for him except that of his honour and dignity.

The angst caused by Raju's confession was reflected in the presentations of the anchors on television channels and the corporate experts they interviewed on that fateful Wednesday. Everybody was aghast. Nobody in their living memory had come across a corporate fraud of such a magnitude in India. There was unanimity that this would have a serious bearing on the image of India as an offshore destination. 'It has taken twenty years for Indian IT companies to build up their reputation and credibility amongst US and European clients. Now in one stroke that credibility is in danger of being lost. It's a huge blow to Indian IT,' said a panellist on a channel. Satyam was compared to Enron, and analysts wondered if the failure of corporate governance meant that there were more Satyams waiting to happen in India.

It was not only Ramalinga Raju who became the object of derision; questions were asked about the auditors who had looked through the accounts of Satyam for so many years and had not detected anything wrong. The integrity of the directors of the board – some of whom were eminent corporate gurus in their own right – was also questioned. 'Was this an effective board or did it consist of sleeping directors only taking their fees and other goodies,' asked someone in the discussion groups.

The internet space was also buzzing with observations. A blogger compared the Satyam empire to a pack of cards whilst another compared it to the movie *Slumdog Millionaire*. 'In *Slumdog Millionaire*, the poor chaiwala knows all the correct answers from his heart and tells them. But nobody believes him; they think he has cheated. Here, the IT czar gives out wrong answers and takes investors up the garden path. But everybody believes him, not realizing that he is cheating,' posted a blogger.

Television anchors were busy berating Raju, but in his native Garagaparru village in the West Godavari district of Andhra Pradesh, people were sympathetic. It was a prosperous village of Rajus where many had made good money by investing in shrimp farming. A part of the profits had been invested in the Satyam scrip. This money was now lost, but the villagers were not angry. Their concern was how the pride of their clan, who had done his primary schooling in the village, would get out of this difficulty. They had reasons for being sympathetic: they believed that Ramalinga was a model citizen, who had invested lakhs in upgrading the social infrastructure of the area through his Byrraju Foundation.

As the day progressed, a clamour to arrest Ramalinga Raju and bring him to book gathered momentum. But if the Andhra Pradesh police had any plans to nab Raju, they were showing no signs of it. The Hyderabad police commissioner, when quizzed by eager media persons, said that he could not arrest Raju for the simple reason that there was no complaint against him. 'On what basis do we take him into custody?' the commissioner asked, hinting that a confession was no proof of Raju's wrongdoing. The national-level agencies, however, seemed to be more receptive: SEBI set up an investigation team to probe the Satyam affair and the ministry of corporate affairs of the Government of India ordered the Registrar of Companies (RoC) to look into Satyam's financial papers.

The political class, however, was silent. Normally quick to comment on matters, politicians seemed to be running for cover that fateful Wednesday. Most of them had lionized Raju and many of them were beneficiaries of largesse and donations from him. They could not berate a man who had been their benefactor. By the end of the day, the beleaguered politicians found a way: they began to express concern for the 50,000-plus employees of Satyam and asserted that jobs would not be lost.

In the afternoon, Ramalinga Raju went to a private guest house in the Jubilee Hills area. He had a rendezvous with an important politician. On the way to the guest house, Raju recalled an incident that took place a few weeks back. K.S. Raju, managing director of Nagarjuna Fertilisers and a friend of Ramalinga, had been sent to jail for not paying interest to some deposit holders from whom the company had borrowed money. A few common friends had approached Ramalinga to help him out. As his nature was never to say no, Ramalinga had met the Andhra Pradesh chief minister, Rajasekhara Reddy, and pleaded with him. As it happened, within days, K.S. Raju was shifted to a private room of a top hospital, supposedly suffering from a heart ailment.

Some important matters were discussed at the meeting between Raju and the leading politician, who gave hope to Raju. 'Don't worry, all the clouds will soon dispel,' the politician told him. Raju came out of the meeting not knowing what the future had in store for him.

Two

An Uproar Nixes a Merger

By the time the presentation was over, Mangalam Srinivasan was very angry. 'You can't treat us as a mere rubber stamp and expect us to say "yes" to whatever you decide. What is the use of having directors like us, when you are not going to consult us at all? And be sure that these comments are recorded in the minutes of the meeting,' she added for good measure. The seventy-year-old lady's rebuke was directed at the senior managers of Satyam, who were trying to sell the idea of merging the IT company with Maytas Infra and Maytas Properties.

Both Ramalinga Raju and his brother, Rama, were missing from the board meeting. 'Both of us have an interest in the proposal of merger because Maytas is also promoted by members of our family. So ladies and gentlemen, if you will permit, we shall keep away from this meeting,' the brothers had said before walking out of Satyam's board room in Hyderabad's Info City, where seven of the nine directors had assembled at 4 p.m. sharp on Thursday, 16 December 2008. The other two directors were not present but were connected through an audio link from the US.

After the brothers had walked out, the other board members decided to appoint Mendu Rammohan Rao, the dean of the Indian School of Business, as the temporary chairman and kick-started the agenda. Rao invited Ram Mynampati, the only full-time director of Satyam, to brief the board about the merger, which was listed as the first item on the agenda for the meeting. In fact, he knew as little about the proposal as did the other directors. Although he was on Satyam's payroll and did not work for anyone else, Mynampati was based in New York. He was responsible for generating business for Satyam in North America and was not involved in corporate decisions of the company. A US citizen, Mynampati had been with Satyam since 1999, but visited Hyderabad only for the company's board meetings, usually held once in two or three months. A few days before this particular board meeting, when Mynampati had reached Hyderabad, Raju told him about the proposal to merge Satyam and Maytas and explained the rationale behind it. It was this spiel that Mynampati – called Ram by his colleagues – started doling out.

'The global meltdown could not have come at a worse time for us. Ninety-five per cent of our clients are in the developed countries and they are the most hit. In this situation, growth is really very, very difficult for us. If we get more business, it will be only if we lower our prices, but that will impact our profitability adversely,' Mynampati explained. He went on, 'The added cause of worry for us is the sort of statements that are coming out of the US about outsourcing. This is clearly a cause for discomfort for us. In these circumstances, there is need for Satyam to diversify. This will be a de-risking policy for the company.' Mynampati concluded, 'Buying into Maytas Infra and Maytas Properties offers a significant opportunity for us. Sectors like infrastructure, energy and irrigation are growing fast and it makes sense for us to diversify into these areas that offer immense possibilities.'

Mynampati had finished but the hardsell continued. Srinivasa Satti, a manager designated as head of mergers and acquisitions, was called in. Satti said the same things that Ram did, further adding hard data to clinch the case. For instance, data showed that India would spend a staggering $430 billion in the next five years in the infrastructure sector, while China would spend $730 billion. This would be a wonderful opportunity to leverage the brand of Satyam and become an eminent player in infrastructure development as well, the manager suggested.

After Satti's presentation was over, the senior vice-president and chief financial officer of Satyam, Srinivasa Vadlamani, came in. He was Satti's boss, but more importantly, he was Raju's right-hand man. Along with Raju, he had over the last one week worked out the exact mechanics of the plan to merge with Maytas. He knew exactly why the merger was being proposed, though the real reasons were not being told to the eminent board. As Raju's closest associate, he knew that Satyam was on the brink of bankruptcy. There was no cash in the coffers of the company, and what was worse, it seemed imminent that this was likely to be found out.

The merger had been proposed as a last-ditch effort to bail out Satyam. With the merger, the financials of Satyam would change: the two companies together would present an entirely different balance sheet. Satyam would temporarily present a pretty picture. This plan had been conjured up after hours of pondering and hushed talks. Now the challenge was to present the proposal to the board of directors in a convincing way. Not that much effort had to be made: the directors were sold on the Satyam magic. Usually they were happy to be on the board, happy to get their remuneration, and assented to every proposal that was made to them.

Vadlamani told the directors that Maytas Properties had already been evaluated by Ernst & Young and that $1.308 billion (Rs 6,410 crore) was a good price to pay for it. Maytas Properties owned 6,800 acres of land across the country, making its land bank one-third the size of DLF. Nearly 245 million square feet of built area could come up on the land owned by Maytas Properties, and at the cost proposed for acquisition, the company would come to Satyam at a steal. Vadlamani also revealed that a price of $306.95 million (Rs 1504.10 crore) was proposed for Maytas Infra, and because it was a publicly listed company, a price of Rs 475 per share (of face value Rs 10) could be paid to acquire the shares from the promoters of the company (that is, the Rajus themselves). For other shareholders not linked with the promoter family, the price offered would be higher at Rs 525 per share.

By the time Vadlamani finished, most of the directors present were more than a little uneasy about what was being said. They had not opened their mouths, because they wanted the presentation to be over. Mangalam Srinivasan was the first to vent her opinion. 'Is there any particular reason – either external or internal – for this initiative and the timing of the proposal?' she asked. Srinivasan, who had been on the board of Satyam for the last seventeen years, knew that there was something amiss. Two and two are not adding to four, she thought and asked for the rationale of the proposal, though Ram, Vadlamani and Satti had explained precisely these things barely a few minutes ago. Mynampati again repeated the explanation.

Rammohan Rao was not a man given to speaking much. A former director of IIM, Bangalore, and recognized as a genius with numbers, Rao asked gently whether this move would not result in diluting the core competency of the company, which lay in the IT business. 'And what are the risks involved in this diversification?' Rao completed his question. Raju's men again repeated the same story – about how a new space was sought to be occupied by the company and how this would not have any impact on the IT business at all. 'Yes, there will be some risks, but they will only be known after we diversify,' Vadlamani proffered.

Vinod Dham, one of the developers of Pentium, and Krishna Palepu, the management guru from Harvard Business School, were clearly not satisfied. The two had been on the board for the last four years, but for this meeting their busy schedules had not allowed them to come all the way from the US to Hyderabad. Palepu knew Raju well. He had been on the board of Vision Compass, a Satyam subsidiary that had been incorporated in the US but which had gone bust. Palepu and Dham had joined via an audio link. 'I am still intrigued about the timing of this event,' Dham commented.

Palepu, who also worked as a consultant for Satyam and was thus not qualified to be called an independent director (as per the company law provisions, he was a non-executive director), had serious concerns. With his vast experience, he knew that shareholders, especially those in North America, would not take very kindly to the proposal. But he stated his concerns very diplomatically. 'You guys have articulated your case very convincingly to us. But remember that investors and analysts in the US will have two serious concerns. First, the proposal to diversify is into unrelated areas, sectors where Satyam does not have any expertise. More importantly, remember this is a related party transaction: the Rajus, who run Satyam, are buying into Maytas, which is promoted by them.' Palepu added, 'You will have to make the same compelling presentation to the investors and make sure that they appreciate that these transactions would enhance Satyam's long-term shareholder value.'

At this point Dham, who had joined the board at Palepu's instance, added, 'Yes, you have to tell the shareholders how the value of their holdings would benefit from this related party transaction.'

Most of the directors were sceptical about the proposal, but two members of the board seemed to have no problems with it. The former cabinet secretary, T.R. Prasad, had joined the Satyam board two years ago after another director of sarkari vintage, V.P. Rama Rao, passed away. Quite unlike other retired bureaucrats, whose preferred destinations are state-owned companies, Prasad joined the boards of many private companies after superannuation. The former babu, who was an IAS officer of the Andhra Pradesh cadre, had had some corporate exposure in Delhi when he was the heavy industries secretary in the mid-1990s. He had dealt with Maruti and had taken up a fight with Suzuki on various issues. The end result was that he was appointed chairman of Maruti Udyog, and his chosen man and fellow Telugu, R.S.S.N.L. Bhaskarudu, was appointed managing director.

At the Satyam board meeting, Prasad was highly appreciative of the diversification plan. 'The Indian economy is growth oriented and the infrastructure sector is clearly seen as a growth story. The Hyderabad metro rail project, which Maytas Infra has been awarded, is four to five times the size of the Bangalore and Hyderabad airport projects, and is in fact the largest BOT [Build, Operate and Transfer] project in the country,' Prasad said. On hearing the price that was being offered to the public shareholders of Maytas Infra, Prasad was appreciative. 'The pricing is very generous, I must admit,' Prasad said.

Professor V.S. Raju, a former director of IIT, Delhi, and a

clansman of Ramalinga Raju, who had been quiet all through, said, 'I also feel that the pricing is very good. I think we should go with the proposal.'

But the temporary chairman of the board, Rammohan Rao, was still not convinced. 'Don't you think we need to ask the management of Maytas whether they are interested in this deal? What are their thoughts on the proposal?' Vadlamani replied that anticipating this question, the top managers of Maytas Infra and Maytas Properties had already been called. In fact, they were waiting in an adjoining conference room. Soon Ramalinga Raju's son, Teja, who was the vice chairman of Maytas Infra, came in along with Mohan Gurunath, the head of strategic planning of the company, and V.V.R. Raju, the chief financial officer. Maytas Infra did not have a managing director. P.K. Madhav, a whole-time director, undertook the responsibilities of managing director. But Madhav was not present at the meeting. He was languishing in jail, arrested on charges of cheating deposit holders of Nagarjuna Finance, a company in which he had worked a couple of years ago. The chairman of the company, R.C. Sinha, was also missing – a retired IAS officer of the Maharashtra cadre, he lived in Mumbai and was unaware of the deal.

The Maytas managers gave the Satyam board the same spiel: how great it would be for both companies to come together, how their synergies would be lead to higher growth for both. After hearing them out, Rammohan Rao asked, 'What about the different work cultures of Satyam and Maytas? Will this not be a problem in the process of integration?' Maytas Infra's CFO, V.V.R. Raju, was quick to respond. 'There wouldn't any problem at all, Sir. The Maytas way is the Satyam way. There is no difference between the two. There are no cultural issues at all. We work in the same way, we follow the same systems,' he said.

Done with Maytas Infra, Satyam's board members called for managers of Maytas Properties. The latter's CEO, K. Thiagrajan, was familiar with Satyam, having served as a manager in the company earlier. He had left a couple of years ago following some differences. But Raju had got him back to Maytas. With Thiagrajan was Badri, the CFO of Maytas Properties. However, conspicuous by his absence was Rama Raju, the younger son of Ramalinga. In his filial love, Raju had not forgotten that his son was still too young and inexperienced to handle the Satyam board.

Though the managers of Maytas Properties also presented a rosy picture of the future of the combined companies, the wizened directors of Satyam were not taken in. There were many questions: which independent agency had valued the assets of Maytas Properties? This was crucial as property prices keep changing. Also, had part of the land assets of Maytas Properties been mortgaged to raise funds from banks and financial institutions? In that case, the value of Maytas Properties would be much less.

'We have got the valuation done, but due to client confidentiality we won't be able to disclose the name of the valuer to the public. However, we can share with you that the valuation has been done by Ernst & Young. They valued the land assets of Maytas Properties at Rs 6,253 crore. Due diligence has also been done by the legal firm Luthra and Luthra, based in Delhi,' Srinivasa Vadlamani answered.

Badri took up the reasoning from here. 'Only 110 acres of the total 6,800 acres owned by the company have been mortgaged to banks and financial institutions. They have been offered as collateral security,' he said.

Even T.R. Prasad, who seemed inclined to favour whatever proposal Satyam's management had made till now, seemed a little sceptical at this juncture. A former land revenue officer who had been a collector in many districts, Prasad knew that land valuation was a tricky business. 'The valuation of Maytas Properties can be done in three distinct categories,' he said. 'Completed projects, for which valuations should be done on actuals; works in progress, for which valuation should be brought in alignment with current market realizations; and land that is awaiting development, for which valuation should be on basic market value at the rates notified by the state government for sale of such lands,' Prasad added. He then sternly pronounced, 'If the valuation of Maytas is significantly higher than the valuation done in the manner that I have suggested, please come back to the board and offer us a full and proper justification for this valuation.'

Other board members agreed and Rammohan Rao summarized that while the Satyam–Maytas deal would appear to add value to Satyam, there was a need to use several methods and many consultants to arrive at a valuation figure. 'There must be complete transparency and justification for the methodology, and these details must be shared with all equity holders,' Rao said.

The meeting was at its conclusive stage. The board decided to give the proposal an in-principle approval, though with the benefit of hindsight, it seems that they should have held back their assent. Rao asked Vadlamani whether it was enough for the board of directors to clear the proposal or would assent by shareholders of Satyam be required as well? The CFO said that board approval would be enough and that there would no need to approach the shareholders. 'In that case, immediately after this board clears the proposal, please inform the stock exchanges, because this information will have a bearing on the stock prices of Satyam,' Rao said. Looking at his watch, the dean of ISB said, 'Well, it is evening, and the Indian bourses are closed for trading for the day. The New York Stock Exchange is yet to open for business. Now is the right time to inform the bourses.' Satyam's company secretary and head of corporate governance, G. Jayaraman, who was present at the meeting but had not spoken a word, nodded his head in agreement and said that this was 'price sensitive information' and that he would immediately inform the stock exchanges. When the board thus cleared the resolution to merge Satyam, Maytas Infra and Maytas Properties, it was 6 p.m.

Little did the directors know that this proposal would have to be reversed within eight hours. Neither did Ramalinga Raju – who came into the board room to greet the board once the meeting got over – realize that the wheels of his destiny had started moving irreversibly and that in another three weeks, he would be in the confines of Hyderabad's Chanchalguda jail.

At 3.45 a.m. the next day, analysts and journalists received a terse SMS from Raju's men: 'We have decided not to move ahead with the acquisition of Maytas in deference to investor community views.' Normally, a board meeting would have to be convened to revoke an earlier decision of the board. But it was late at night and an emergency decision had to be taken. Raju informed board members – on email – that he would have to take such a decision immediately. A formal approval was to be obtained from the board at its next meeting. In the event, Raju did not wait for replies to come before informing the NYSE that the plan was off.

Not that Raju had any choice, faced with the kind of investor fury that he was. On the NYSE, trading on the Satyam scrip had to be suspended indefinitely after it lost 52 per cent of its value as the ADR plummeted. Fifty-eight per cent of Satyam's equity was held by foreign institutional investors (FII) and they were angry. These were the investors who had pumped in considerable amounts of cash into Satyam, seeing the company as a growth stock. But they felt betrayed by this move. They clearly saw that there was a game on, though they did not realize that Satyam was tottering on the brink with no cash reserves.

The FIIs, mostly based in the US or UK but with regional headquarters in Singapore and Hong Kong, saw this as an attempt to palm off the two Maytas companies that were owned by the Rajus to Satyam, a company that was largely owned by public shareholders. Since Satyam would acquire Maytas at a price ($1.6 billion), they perceived the money as being transferred to the Rajus, who owned Maytas. This was not Raju's gameplan, but the investors had no idea that Satyam's books were all cooked up. 'We will take all it does to see that the proposal is reversed,' declared many FII representatives on television channels, which started buzzing the moment news about the merger proposal was out.

Other business analysts feared that it was a trick to lend the Satyam name to Maytas. Satyam had a brand image whereas Maytas was little known beyond Hyderabad and Andhra Pradesh. However, Maytas was in need of moolah because it had been awarded the Rs 12,500-crore Hyderabad metro rail project. Since Satyam was a well-known name on the bourses, money could be raised from the market in its name through both loans and equity. While nobody would lend a penny to Maytas in these days of slowdown, if Satyam and Maytas became one, there would be no problem, said these analysts. Whatever be the case, investment analysts and general business analysts openly expressed their disapproval of the merger proposal.

Raju reversed his own proposal, but that was not enough to douse the dissatisfaction of the analysts. When the Indian bourses opened for trade a couple of hours after Raju's SMS was sent, the investors were still very angry. 'How can we trust a company whose board allows a deal designed to benefit the Rajus? This is a total breakdown of corporate governance. Who knows what they will do in the future? This time around they have rescinded the deal. But the fact of the matter is that they did conceive of such an idea.' These were the sort of comments that were heard from analysts and investors, some of whom even talked of changing the management of the company: 'If Ramalinga Raju can plot this, owning barely 8 per cent of the equity of Satyam, imagine what he can do if he owns more? He has clearly lost public trust.'

It was not merely Raju and Satyam who faced a crisis of confidence; the independent directors of the company were also under attack. 'Are they *khao peeo, mast ho jao* type of directors?' asked Monotosh Sinha, then executive director of a leading brokering firm. 'They are independent directors only in name, in reality they are dependent directors who have been compromised by Satyam's management. They should be sacked immediately for not discharging their role with adequate responsibility,' remarked stockbrokers on Dalal Street and other financial analysts.

Consequently, Satyam's scrip tanked on the National and Bombay Stock Exchange, falling 30 per cent. The share closed at Rs 158.05, which was a fifty-two-week low. Later in the day, Ramalinga Raju issued a statement even as his flunkeys held a press conference to explain the aborted deal. Raju's statement was a repeat of the story fed to the board of directors the previous day: how the acquisitions would have paved the way for accelerated growth in additional geographies and market segments, and how it would de-risk the core business by bootstrapping a new business vertical. Vadlamani confessed at the press conference: 'We never anticipated the reaction that would be generated by the move…we underestimated it…we thought we could manage it.' And Ram Mynampati tried to make light of the situation: 'It was a judgement call and sometimes some judgements do not turn out to be good.'

Significantly, even after being faced with investor wrath, Vadlamani continued to lie. 'The deal had been in the offing for long and we looked at many companies for acquisition. But ultimately our choice fell on Maytas Properties. The primary reason for this is that the company had zero debt. It has not borrowed from the market. Some of the other companies at which we were looking have huge debts to public,' he said. This was a plain lie because the proposal was to cover up the situation in Satyam. No other company had been considered for acquisition.

Although nobody at that point knew why Raju was doing what he was, a ton of bricks seemed to have fallen on him. Faced with the situation, Raju did what he was best at – he shut himself up at his home, trying to figure out ways to get out of this mess. He made several calls to financiers and politicians who, he felt, could bail him out with cash. But nobody was in a position to help him. Meanwhile, Satyam's scrip was continually being battered on the bourses and the public outcry was intensifying.

If this wasn't bad enough, worse was to follow. On 23 December, news flashed across television channels that Satyam had been blacklisted by the World Bank. The reason was that Satyam had made 'improper benefits to the Bank staff' and that there was 'lack of transparency on invoices'. Stated in simpler terms, this meant that Satyam had bribed some officials of World Bank to land a contract. This information seemed to confirm acts of wrongdoing by the company. There seemed no end to Satyam's woes.

Instances of other frauds allegedly committed by the company started coming out in public. The British online and mobile payment services, Upaid, filed a suit in Texas district court in the US seeking an immediate deposition by Ramalinga Raju, Srinivasa Vadlamani and G. Jayaraman on the Satyam–Maytas proposal. A case filed earlier by Upaid contending that Satyam had sold Upaid's intellectual property and products was already being fought in the same court. In another twist, director Krishna Palepu got a mail from someone who refused to reveal his identify. The person said that he was an employee of Satyam and asserted that the account books of the company were fudged. Shocked by the contents, Palepu forwarded the mail to Rammohan Rao. The ISB dean in turn circulated it amongst all directors on the board. But everyone kept quiet. The opinion of the auditors was also sought, but to no effect.

The real shocker, however, came on Christmas Day, when Mangalam Srinivasan, who had been upset with the way the merger proposal with Maytas had been rammed through, decided to quit the board. In her home town, Bangalore, since the board meeting, the lady, who had once been offered the job of scientific advisor to the government by Indira Gandhi, threw in the towel after agonizing for many days. 'I am left with no option but to resign with immediate effect. I had raised many issues related to procedures and had expressed reservations during the board meeting. I had not cast a dissenting vote against the deal for which I take moral responsibility,' Srinivasan said in a fax message from Bangalore. A copy of the communication was leaked to sections of the media before she took the next flight out of India.

Srinivasan's resignation put pressure on the other board members of Satyam, and more importantly, on Raju and his men. Anticipating further trouble if the board members got together, Raju postponed to 10 January a meeting that was slated three days later. The ostensible reason cited was that two overseas directors, Krishna Palepu and Vinod Dham, wanted to attend the meeting to sort out the company's problems but were unable to make it at such a short notice. The other directors, however, had begun to mull whether they should continue on the board. They were faced with public recriminations, and some ministers of the union government had also started calling the independent directors the laughing stock of the nation. Most under attack was ISB's dean, Rammohan Rao, who had chaired the crucial board meeting on 16 December.

T.R. Prasad, who had supported the move to merge Satyam and Maytas, remained unfazed, however. 'I cannot sacrifice the interests of the 52,000 employees of Satyam by leaving. I cannot desert the ship at such a crucial time,' Prasad said in press interviews from his home in Vishakapatnam, 650 kilometres away from Hyderabad.

The board meeting that was deferred had been called for considering a buyback of the shares of Satyam. This meant that the company would acquire its own shares from shareholders who were not happy with what was going on; obviously, this was with a view to quell investor dissatisfaction. By deferring the meeting, the Rajus bought time because Satyam anyway did not have the cash to buy back the shares.

With pressure mounting, Raju also agreed to appoint DSP Merrill Lynch as advisors to recommend what additional moves the company could make to address investor dissatisfaction. Investors were pointing fingers at 'sleeping directors', so DSP was specifically asked to recommend, on an emergency basis, ways to strengthen its board by altering its size and composition. The consultant was given only ten days to submit its report.

But the fire had come to rage in Satyam. No step would be enough to take care of the problems of the beleaguered company, it seemed. Adding fuel to the fire, Vinod Dham and Krishna Palepu decided to quit the board on 27 December. Dham, a hardcore technology man, had got some independent investigations done and was fully convinced that Satyam's account books were fudged. There was no way that he would sit on the board any longer. He in turn convinced Palepu, and both of them informed Raju that they were leaving.

Meanwhile, along with investor demand for better corporate governance, employee dissatisfaction was also on the rise, what with words like 'change in management' and 'induction of a strategic investor' in the air. In fact, the employees of the company were gripped by a sense of uncertainty, especially as recession was slowly but surely setting in. This meant that business would be bad and there would not be many jobs going around. Raju, who had been hoodwinking his stakeholders all these years, realized that things would go out of hand if he did not calm the employees, who formed the backbone of the IT company.

On 30 December, Raju wrote to all the associates in the company exhorting them 'to disbelieve all the wild speculation and unchecked rumours' that were going around and 'stay focused on consumers and continue to focus on bringing about stakeholder delight'. Raju claimed that customers continued to show a very high level of trust in Satyam and the steps being taken to regain the confidence of investors. This, he said, was being attempted by changing the size and composition of the board, thereby strengthening it. Raju also stressed that Merrill Lynch had been engaged to provide strategic advice and options. He also reminded his staff that the Satyam–Maytas deal was cleared unanimously by the high-profile board of Satyam. Of course, he forgot to mention that three of the board members had already quit in disgust.

Not sure how much of an impact his mail would have on his employees, Ramalinga Raju got his brother Rama to send another mail the following day, which was New Year's Eve. Ramu wrote in his mail, aptly titled 'Goodbye 2008, Welcome 2009':

'Let the events of the last two weeks not cloud our view of the entire calendar year.' He went on to remind the employees that 2008 was the year when Satyam had crossed a turnover of $2 billion. It had also seen three strategic acquisitions overseas and secured the contract to partner with FIFA to provide IT services for the World Cup in 2010 and 2014. Rama also pointed out that Satyam had become the first Indian company to get listed on the Euronext exchange.

All this, however, did little to soothe the nerves of the employees, and this was not the least because on 29 December, Raju had written to the Bombay and National Stock Exchange that the 'company's promoters [that is, the Rajus themselves] had pledged their entire shareholdings to institutional investors who may exercise or may have exercised' their option to sell it off. In simple language, this meant that the Rajus had mortgaged their shares in Satyam to banks to raise funds for various activities.

With the share market crashing and Satyam's scrip falling, the banks had told the Rajus that the shares they held as mortgage were not enough to cover their collateral value. The only way they could save these shares was to pay up cash to cover for the depreciated collateral. But the Rajus had no cash, so the banks had no option but to sell the shares to make up for their losses. And this is what they did.

As the old year gave way to the new, it became clear that Ramalinga Raju was in real trouble and that his company, the fourth-largest IT firm in the country, was a distressed asset. Raju was the promoter of Satyam, but his shareholding and that of his family members had fallen to a little over 2 per cent. It was as if Satyam had been orphaned.

THREE

A Scheme Is Hatched

On 6 December 2008, the Hyderabad chapter of the CEO Club (India) held an interactive session with Ramalinga Raju. Ironically, the subject of the interaction was 'Secrets of Success: Lessons Learnt From Life'. By this time Raju was already in a crisis – this was barely ten days before his last-ditch effort to merge Maytas and Satyam. Raju had wanted to wriggle out of the session but could not, having committed to it earlier. Most of the members of the club were personally known to him. They would not listen to his request to excuse him from the well-publicized meeting.

But the worries showed on the face of the usually calm and collected Raju at the meeting that day. Maybe the subject had something to do with his discomfiture, and in what was a Freudian slip, Raju at one point in the course of the interaction remarked: 'Why should somebody share his secret of success with anybody else?' A CEO present at the meeting says: 'I was stunned to hear him. He was not known to talk like this. But now I know why he must have been so uncomfortable.'

All through the proceedings that day, Raju rambled and was hardly ever on the subject – he was most probably thinking about how to bail himself out. But there was no solution in sight. Nobody was ready to lend him the sum that he needed to save himself. Without this money he was doomed, and he was well aware of this.

The monsoon season in the Deccan extends from July to September, but the rains start abating by the middle of September. However, the ides of September in 2008 had brought troubles for Raju in his finest hour. After the contract (known in technical parlance as 'concession' agreement) for executing the Hyderabad metro rail was signed – a project whose successful completion would catapult Raju into a much bigger league (somebody had remarked that he was on the way to become the new Nizam of Hyderabad) – both the stock market and the realty market had started collapsing.

Satyam's stock, which ruled at Rs 490 per share in the first week of June, had come down to Rs 418 by the middle of August and Rs 335 by 18 September. By the end of September, it had crashed to Rs 298. This had serious implications for Raju, who had pledged his entire holding of over 8.62 per cent of the equity – the shares that he held in his name and that of his wife, and in the names of his brother Rama and his wife.

These shares were pledged to borrow money from banks and financial institutions. The problem, however, was that the shares had been pledged two years earlier, when the share value of Satyam was much higher, at over Rs 800 per share. As per the norms of the financial markets, if share prices plummeted below the level at which they had been pledged, the borrower has to make good the loss by pledging more shares or paying up in cash. But Raju had no more shares – he had pledged his entire shareholding. And what was worse, he had no cash, for the amount that had been raised from the mortgage had been spent on buying up land and real estate. In fact, he had borrowed large sums of money from the market using his reputation and creditworthiness. But he now needed more money to save himself from lenders and save Satyam for himself.

Raju faced a double whammy: the real estate market had also begun crashing. The US subprime crisis had hit the Indian shores. After remaining flat for a year from June 2007 to June 2008, the real estate market had gone under. This was in defiance of expectations: the consensus at the beginning of the year was that property prices would continue to be flat and a dip, if any, would only be marginal. What certainly had Raju more worried was the fact that the fall in prices was the highest in areas of Hyderabad such as Medchal, Nizampet, Miyapur and Bachupally, where his companies held large chunks of land. This meant that he could not even sell his land and hope to at least break even.

Raju also knew that while the general public was oblivious to whatever was happening around them, operators in the real estate market were shrewd. They had their ear close to the ground and picked up the smallest bits of gossip and information relating to realty. Raju was a big operator and if the market perceived that he was making distress sales, the news was likely to spread like bush fire. Having no other option, Raju did try to sell off a few plots of land, albeit discreetly. But he was unable to do so. With prices expected to go down further, there were no buyers.

Raju must have cursed his luck, and wondered why he had purchased land at exorbitant rates in the outlying areas of Hyderabad. Why had he believed the neo realty experts (who had come up in the aftermath of liberalization and had their own logic about the land market)? They had told him that buying land at more than the market price would push up the prices in the surrounding areas. These experts, who were well acquainted with the workings of the stock market, had also told Raju that a realty company could do well on the bourses only if it had a huge land bank.

'They don't see how many projects you have successfully developed. They only look at the projects that you have in hand and the land that you control. This is the key to good valuation,' the analysts had told him. They had cited the example of DLF, by far the biggest realty player in India, which was engaged in a similar exercise.

'Raju got taken in because he was keen to do a public issue for Maytas Properties, a company that he wanted to promote for his younger son, Rama Raju Jr (who was still in his twenties and had returned after an MBA from Carnegie Mellon),' says a leading realtor of Hyderabad, who has seen Raju in action. He adds: 'It is a result of this thinking that Raju was frantically buying land – at whatever price he was able to – through Maytas Properties and the 327 privately owned companies that he controlled.'

The realtor reveals that younger brother Rama had cautioned Raju against going all out to buy land at whatever price it was available. But the voice of sanity had been lost on him, not the least because elder son Teja Raju was bullish. Two years older than Rama Jr and also holding a master's degree from the US, Teja was handling Maytas Infra, which, as the name suggests, was in the business of construction and implementing infrastructure projects. Teja was impetuous and assertive and kept the company of the sons of top industrialists. Rama, who respected Raju, had given up and gone along with him. But it had now landed Raju in a mess.

Raju did not know what to do next. Would he have to offload shares that he and his family members owned in Maytas Infra?

Maytas Infra had raised funds through a public issue a year ago and his kith and kin owned a large percentage of shares in the company.

It was in this frame of mind that Raju went to New Delhi to attend the meeting of the India Economic Summit of the World Economic Forum on 16 November 2008. Again, this was a meeting that Raju could not afford to miss: he was a co-chairman at one of the conference meets. Moreover, the meeting offered him a chance to meet top-level officials from the government and the corporate sector and also foreign contacts. If nothing else, the summit would give him an insight into the slowdown that had set in in the Indian economy.

In the course of the meetings in New Delhi, Raju did not betray any obvious sign of nervousness, at least in public. He gave his trademark spiel: 'Competitiveness will be the key driver, protectionism will be dangerous if it comes in the way of entrepreneurship...As India addresses the negative effects of the global financial crisis, coping with the problem is not the issue, it is the uncertainty of not understanding the extent of the problem.' Those privy to his affairs say that his private meetings with fellow businessmen and top government guns did not give him any confidence. None of them seemed optimistic. They all felt that this was just the beginning and that the worst would come after March. 'It will trough out in the middle of 2009. Normal situation can be expected after Diwali 2009,' the industrialists said. Raju realized he was hurtling towards a major crisis.

Eleven days earlier, on 5 November, Satyam had been honoured as the most admired knowledge enterprise and the award was given out at the CII knowledge summit in Mumbai. Barely two days later, Raju was in Kuala Lumpur to receive an award for corporate governance from Frost and Sullivan. Raju had many fans in Kuala Lumpur, where Satyam had an office.

The Malays thought that Raju was an icon of the developing world and someone worth emulating. To coincide with the trip, Satyam had bought out a Motorola outfit with 150 employees in Cyberjaya. In fact, Satyam was in the process of developing a fifteen-acre information technology campus in Malaysia, called the Super Corridor. Even in Kuala Lumpur, Raju tried to approach corporate honchos for help but with his usual communication problems, found it difficult to make himself understood.

On his way back from New Delhi, Raju's mind was active. Was there any way in which he could raise more funds from Satyam? But that was not an option at all. For the last seven years he had been falsifying the accounts of Satyam to inflate its turnover and profits. So Satyam did not have as much in its banks as was projected. Moreover, the impact of the slowdown in the US would affect the Indian IT sector the most. Companies with declining profitability and falling revenues in the US would cut their IT spending. Also, the increasing outcry against outsourcing and shipping of jobs overseas was likely to impact Satyam as well. This in turn could well result in a fall in the company's share prices, making Raju even more vulnerable.

Raju wondered what his peers in the IT industry would do if they were faced with a problem like this. For example, what would Azim Premji do if he had a cash problem? Raju thought of Premji because, of all IT companies, Wipro was a family-run set-up like his. Tata Consultancy Services and Infosys could not be compared with Satyam. Raju knew Premji quite well and admired his smartness. But then, as he reflected, Raju must have realized that even Wipro was not comparable with Satyam. Premji held more than 80 per cent of the company and here he did not own even 8 per cent.

Reflecting on his practices, Raju realized that he had begun fudging also because he was trying to compete with Wipro and Infosys. The practice of declaring quarterly results had put pressure on companies to demonstrate shining results. In the software industry, Infosys was the first company to declare its results on the seventh day of every quarter. 'I now understand that Raju would see the Infosys results and then fudge his accounts so that it looked at least a bit like Narayana Murthy and Nilekani's company,' says the chief financial officer of a leading company in Hyderabad. Satyam invariably declared its results on the seventeenth day of the quarter.

Even as all this went through his mind, Raju thought of the email that he had written to his staff a month ago, on 15 October, to bolster their morale, while himself drawing comfort from the words: 'We faced a similar situation after 9/11…I am sure we can overcome the present crisis too…do not panic…work hard and let's face the challenge together.' He also thought about the message that he and his managers had been giving out to the media in the last few months about how Satyam was protected against the crisis. Raju had himself said that Satyam's business model was robust and free of risk and that Satyam's growth was broad-based and not dependent on specific sectors or customers. CFO Srinivasa Vadlamani had told the media that the recession in the US had not hit the orders of Satyam in Europe. Moreover, the recession had only led to some cancellations in the banking and financial services (BFIS) space. There was strong demand still in the US from the retail, engineering and pharmacy sectors.

Though Satyam was the immediate problem, Raju's troubles also lay elsewhere – the metro rail project for Hyderabad that he had taken on. To begin with, Maytas would have to cough up Rs 230 crore as performance guarantee for the project. However, he had time till March 2009 to deposit this amount. What was worrying him was his immediate requirement of funds.

Raju's mind again went back to Maytas Infra. For the record, the Rajus owned 36.84 per cent of its equity. But Raju knew that in reality they owned much more. In fact, the family controlled another 46.53 per cent of the equity. Thus the family's total holding in Maytas Infra was nearly 84 per cent. A part of the shares was pledged to financial institutions, but taking advantage of the provisions of company law, not all the shares had been shown as owned by the promoters. Rama Raju owned 8.74 per cent of the equity of Maytas Infra, his wife Radha had 2.35 per cent, brother Suryanarayana had 4.30 per cent of the equity and his wife Jhansi Rani had 2.35 per cent. But the promoter of the company on paper was Teja Raju, and there was nothing in law that said the shareholdings of his uncles Rama and Suryanarayana and aunt Jhansi would have to be clubbed with his shareholdings.

Two other privately owned companies run by the family had nearly 17 per cent of the equity of Maytas Infra. Raju thought that if nothing else worked out, they would have to get rid of Maytas Infra shares. However, the idea of doing so pained him: the company had just done a public issue barely a year ago but its order books, which included many road, irrigation and power projects spread across various states of India, were full. It had been named as the fastest growing construction company in the country and what was more, it had its sights set on big business. Only a few weeks back, Maytas had spawned a subsidiary for the business of prospecting, exploring and operating iron ore mines and the manufacture of iron and steel products.

The company was a father's gift to his son, and Raju did not want to dilute the shareholding in Maytas and make it slide like Satyam. Let me consider the option of divesting from Maytas a little later, Raju told himself, even as he realized that Maytas Infra, by and large, had been spared the vicissitudes of the market

– its scrip was actually crawling up. From an average price of Rs 421 in July, the Rs 10 scrip had climbed to Rs 495 in October.

This was, of course, largely because the Rajus themselves owned 84 per cent of the company, which meant that only 16 per cent was in the market. The Rajus had not sold their shares, so the price of the scrip had been maintained on Dalal Street. The share was listed on the bourses on 25 September 2007 at a price of Rs 370 (its face value was Rs 10), a handsome gain for a new company. If the Raju family equity was diluted to, say, 50 per cent, the share value would be much less. This would not only reduce the wealth of the Rajus, it would also reduce their ability to raise funds from the market. Lenders loaned money based on the value of the shares that you presented to them as collaterals. If the value was less, lenders would only offer you a proportionate amount.

On reaching Hyderabad, the first thing Raju did was to take an inventory of the land he controlled, say advisors close to him. He had land not only in Hyderabad, but in Chennai, Bangalore and Nagpur as well. Most of the land was in the name of the 327 privately owned companies floated by Raju, and Raju's guess was that it totalled over 6,500 acres. Though there was nothing benami about them, the public had no idea about the existence of these companies. Raju was not going to disclose the information, though sharp investors, who had gone through all the documents of Maytas, would already have a clue about it.

Mercifully, most of these privately owned companies had loose agreements with Maytas Properties to develop the land. So a private consultant could be roped in to certify Maytas Properties' landholdings, or what could be shown as its landholdings. Technically, this was not correct because Maytas Properties had only development rights – the land was held by the 327 companies. The consultants could be persuaded to provide the certification, the IT czar figured. After interacting with the upwardly mobile business crowd that went to Davos to participate in the meetings of the World Economic Forum (WEF), Raju knew that the bigger the consultant who gave him a certificate, the better for him. He would tell his managers to talk to one of the big four consultants in the country, he decided.

Once he had a certified land bank in the name of Maytas Properties, Raju could find ways of leveraging it to raise funds. The best way, of course, would be to do a public issue. That is what he had conceived of a long time ago but it was not feasible at the time what with the stock market on a downward journey. From 17,648 on the last day of January 2008 it had gone down to 13,461 on the last day of June. At the end of November, it was down to 9,092. So where was the question of a public issue now? No private investor would be willing to infuse funds into Maytas Properties either. Wall Street had collapsed, and along with it all dreams of private funds.

A few months ago, however, Raju had managed to reach an agreement with a private equity fund in the US to infuse Rs 600 crore into Maytas Properties. This had been done through the good offices of Nimesh Kampani, a leading stockbroker on Dalal Street who had diversified into the business of financing companies. But that was then. Nimesh Kampani was himself in trouble now, finding himself in a tangle with the Andhra Pradesh government.

It was the beginning of December by now. Raju had come to realize that nobody would be willing to bail him out. He really would have to think of innovative ways of keeping out of harm's way. Of course, the option of divesting from Maytas Infra was still there. He started holding brainstorming meetings with top executives of Maytas to figure out if they could offer any way out. Needless to say, Raju talked vaguely at these sessions because he could not afford to tell these managers what the problem was. The result was expected: no solution seemed forthcoming.

Raju now began a series of in-depth consultations with his brother Rama. He was the only man who knew all his secrets. A couple of days later, Raju could see light at the end of the tunnel. 'How about merging Maytas and Satyam?' he asked Rama. 'That way the entire problem can be solved at one stroke. Satyam could acquire Maytas on the grounds of diversification. The software sector is facing bad days, but the infrastructure sector, dependent on government funding and plan allocations, is still very much kicking. And it would remain so because the slowdown has not affected the government sector,' Raju concluded.

Satyam was short on cash in its books by Rs 7,000 crore. If Satyam could buy Maytas for more than this sum and not pay for it, then the hole in the books would be covered and there would be more cash in hand. Of course, a book-keeping transfer would have to be shown, but this would be only a paper entry; no cash would actually change hands, at least immediately. The Maytas shareholders would not object: 84 per cent of the shares were owned by Raju's family members. Maytas was listed on the bourses as a public limited company; in reality, it was run as a privately owned company. After considerable thought, Rama agreed that for the moment this was the only course available. Raju felt relieved.

Thus began another phase of frenzied activity in Satyam, Maytas Infra and Maytas Properties. Trusted senior staff were called separately and briefed. They were told to get ready and prepare for a presentation at a board meeting that was slated for 16 December, where the merger of Satyam and the two Maytas companies would be formally proposed. The only brief that Raju gave these managers was to somehow present the transaction as being worth $1.6 billion. In other words, Satyam would consider buying Maytas Infra and Maytas Properties for $1.6 billion.

Raju did not explain to his men the rationale for arriving at this figure. But there was a rationale: with the dollar hovering around Rs 48, $1.6 billion would translate to Rs 7,680 crore. That would cover up the hole in Satyam and leave some cash to spare. The hole was worth Rs 7,136 crore: Rs 5,040 crore in non-existent cash or bank balances, Rs 376 crore in non-existent interest, Rs 1,230 crore in understated liabilities and Rs 490 crore in overstated debtors' position. But Raju, though a gambler by instinct, did not want to leave anything to chance. He thought that it would be good to keep some more cash ready.

So while midnight oil was being burnt at the office of Maytas Infra in Begumpet area of Hyderabad, Raju finally decided to shed some equity of the company for this ready cash. Since selling off these shares, labelled as promoters' equity, would spark off market rumours and lead to a hammering of the shares, Raju felt that the safest bet would be to get rid of shares that belonged to his family members but were not listed as promoters' shareholding. Accordingly, the shares of Radha Raju, the wife of Rama Raju, which accounted for 4.38 per cent of the equity, were offloaded and Rama Raju's 8.74 per cent was pledged to raise funds. Of course, even this move had its downside: the higher the floating per cent of the Maytas share in the company, the less control the Rajus would have over market forces. But all this was required for the growth and consolidation of Raju's empire.

Meanwhile, Srinivasa Vadlamani, Raju's humble comrade-in-arms, came back and told him that the valuation of Maytas was proving to be difficult: the sum total of the value of Maytas Infra and Maytas Properties was not adding up to $1.6 billion. The problem was that Maytas Infra was listed on the market, so its valuation had to be transparent and based on the ruling scrip prices of the company. Of course, some margin could be given for the fact that after obtaining the contract for Hyderabad's rail project, the company had gone up in public estimation. Even the WEF had recognized the potential of Maytas Infra and had granted it membership as a global growth company. That made Maytas Infra the only infrastructure company from India to be admitted to the WEF.

But in spite of this, there was a limit to which the valuation of Maytas Infra could be raised on the pretext that it had a higher brand value. The only jugglery that could be done was with the valuation of Maytas Properties. 'So go ahead, what's stopping you?' said Raju. He added: 'Unlike stock prices, there is no index for land prices. So you can assume it to be anything so long as it does not appear unreasonable. Instead of the present prices, you can choose to take the prices prevailing six months ago. Anyway, most of our land is in upcoming or prime areas,' Raju argued, or so claim members of his team.

Vadlamani nodded and went away. The next day he came back to say that everything had been done. Maytas Properties had development rights to 6,500 acres of land, and this had been valued at Rs 6,500 crore. This meant Rs 1 crore per acre, which was not unreasonable. Vadlamani later told him that the services of Ernst & Young had been availed of for evaluation of the landholdings. A Delhi-based law firm, Luthra & Luthra, had also been retained. The two consultants had, however, not been told the purpose for which their advice was sought. They were totally in the dark, but they had not asked too many questions. They had gone around their job in a professional manner.

Raju was now very relaxed. He was smiling at what he thought was a brilliant gameplan. Raju remembered how in September, after the last quarterly results of Satyam were announced, analysts had asked tough questions about the company's financials. One particular analyst, Raju recollected, wanted to know why Satyam kept so much cash – upwards of Rs 1,700 crore – in a current account, which did not earn any interest at all. Wasn't this poor financial management? Who in his senses would do such a thing?

Vadlamani had proffered some garbled explanation and saved the day, but from that day Raju had been alive to the possibility of his being found out. After all he could not tell the analyst that this Rs 1,700 crore was a fictitious amount; it did not exist at all. Raju suspected that some of his top managers had an inkling that something was amiss in Satyam. What else would account for the fact that so many of his senior managers were seeking to divest shares in the company that had been given to them as employee stock option?

Though Raju was more relaxed than before, worries periodically kept coming back. He knew that the independent directors on the board of Satyam could be convinced. But the tribe of inquisitive analysts was a problem. They would immediately jump to the conclusion that this was a misuse of the surpluses of Satyam (that rightfully belonged to the shareholders) to buy Maytas, in which the Rajus had a higher shareholding. A lot of effort would be required to convince them that there was nothing amiss. Little did they know that Maytas would be bought for free.

In the midst of this plan, another thought crossed Raju's mind, and he immediately called Vadlamani to his room. 'Please look up the company law books and ensure that the directors don't ask for shareholders' approval for the merger. Tell them that the law is clear and the approval of directors is enough to clear the proposal,' Raju told him. Vadlamani understood, as always, and walked out of the room.

Though a student of commerce and management, Raju was fascinated by physics and science fiction. Isaac Asimov's books were a tension buster for him and Einstein's theory of relativity and the structure of space and time always set him thinking. Raju's mind went back to Einstein. Two events, simultaneous for some observers, may not be simultaneous for another, if the observers are in relative motion. According to Einstein, nothing in this universe could travel faster than light. If it did, time would start moving backwards. And if time could move backwards, there was nothing that was fixed in this universe. In other words, there was nothing black and white; everything was in shades of grey. There was no absolute truth, no absolute *Satyam*.

Raju also recollected the three laws of robots that Asimov had propounded. The first law: A robot may not injure a human being or through interaction allow a human being to come to harm. The second law: A robot must obey any orders given to it by human beings, except when such order came into conflict with the first law. And the third law: A robot must protect its own existence as long as such protection does not conflict with the first and second laws. Raju thought of himself as a robot who had not harmed anyone.

FOUR

The Journey to the Top

By the time Raju went to jail, he had become a confident man of the world – he knew how to get public sympathy even as he was found breaking the law. But it had not always been like this. When he embarked on his career, Raju was confused like any other young man. Returning to India in 1977 after completing MBA from Ohio University, Raju hadn't a clue about what to do in life. Some friends told him that there was a part-time teaching job being offered in the Administrative Staff College of India. But Raju's father, who called the shots at home, told him to forget self-doubts and focus on the family business.

Primarily agriculturists, with about 100 acres of land in native Bhimavaram (400 km from Hyderabad) and other neighbouring places and twenty acres of grape farms around Hyderabad, the family had diversified into the hospitality industry. Ramalinga's grandfather, Rama Raju, died around this time and the young man was handed over a property called Dhanunjaya Hotels

Private Limited. He didn't make any success of this and the floundering company was sold off a few years later.

In the early 1980s, Dhirubhai Ambani's Reliance and Vimal had suddenly broken into the Indian corporate scene. With his native intelligence, Ambani had realized that there was a market in India for nylons, polyester and other synthetic textiles that were till then available only abroad. To satisfy this craze for 'smuggled' textiles, Ambani started producing them in India, sparking off not only consumer interest but also the curiosity of other potential producers.

Raju felt that textiles could be a good business to venture into. Fortune smiled on him in the form of Prime Minister Indira Gandhi. After being routed in the 1977 elections and losing her Rae Bareli seat, Mrs Gandhi had shifted to the Medak constituency near Hyderabad for a berth in the Lok Sabha. Though close to the capital of Andhra Pradesh, the district was very backward. On her instructions – after she became prime minister once again in 1980 – the state government began to aggressively promote industries in the backward district. So when Raju applied for a licence in 1981 to set up a synthetic yarn manufacturing unit called Sri Satyam Spinning Mills, the Andhra Pradesh State Industrial Development Corporation (APSIDC) was ready to partly bankroll the project. But Raju had not yet learnt the ropes of business and the company could just manage to trot along.

In late 1986, the Government of India announced its first software export policy, and it was at this time that Ramalinga's country cousin, D.V.S. Raju, returned from the US. He had also gone to Ohio University, to study electronics engineering. D.V.S. Raju told Ramalinga that setting up an IT company would not be a bad idea. Having stayed in the West himself and thus been exposed to the trends in the developed world, Raju was quick to appreciate the proposal and thus the foundation for Satyam Computer Services was laid. Starting with twenty employees, the company began operations from a small office in P&T Colony in Secunderabad on 6 June 1987. Not well versed with IT, Raju gave the charge of the company to D.V.S. Raju and himself continued to concentrate on the yarn mill, though it was going nowhere. A year later, another company was spawned after Dhanunjaya Hotels was sold off. The charge of this new company, called Satyam Constructions, was vested with Ramalinga's younger brother, Rama, who had just returned from the US, having done an MBA from Loredo State University in Texas.

In a couple of years, Satyam Computers had moved to a bigger office at Mayfair building in the Begumpet area of Hyderabad, but the company was still not very stable. It required frequent cash infusions. K.B.K. Raju, the promoter of the Nagarjuna group and the most prosperous businessman in the Raju community, bailed out the company a few times.

But Satyam soon got going with the acquisition of a US customer. John Deere, a well-known tractor company based in Chicago, engaged Satyam to develop some software for its operations. In those days, software developers typically worked out of the client's office in what was essentially an onshore model. This was largely because clients wanted to be taken through each phase of the software development. Satyam proposed that its software engineers would work offshore – from India. This would lead to considerable cost advantages: obviously because engineers in India would have to be paid much less than if they were based out of the US. But John Deere's management would not agree. The Rajus, however, persisted and proposed an alternate model for the purposes of demonstration – they put up thirty-five Satyam engineers in a Chicago building across the road from the John Deere plant for three months. At night, these Satyam engineers would upload the developed software into John Deere's mainframe computers using a satellite link through a 64-bps line. The experiment was a fantastic success, and John Deere's managers realized that offshore operations were far superior to an onsite exercise. Thus Satyam became the pioneer of outsourcing from India and was allowed to develop the software in its offices in India.

The first-ever outsourcing contract tested Raju's abilities to liaise with the powers that be to the hilt. To obtain permission from the Government of India was a difficult job. The babus he had to deal with initially thought that he was trying to send off secret information abroad, but the intervention of a fellow Andhraite, Hanuman Chowdhry, who was chairman of the Videsh Sanchar Nigam Limited, ultimately helped Raju obtain the necessary clearances.

Buoyed by the offshoring experiment, Ramalinga Raju felt confident and decided that the time was ripe for a public issue. It was 1992, and Harshad Mehta was rampaging on Dalal Street. Stories started doing the rounds about how you could double or treble your wealth on the stockmarket in a matter of a few days. Raju was not willing to let go of the opportunity. The initial public issue of Satyam was a grand success (like all share issues were in those heady days) and was oversubscribed seventeen times. Ramalinga Raju became the chairman of the company. Before this, Ramalinga was only the vice-chairman and had left the operations largely to D.V.S. Raju. The latter had a stake in the company but was more focussed on the technical side. Though not hands-on, Ramalinga had helped in people management and other issues related to human resources and corporate relations, including government dealings.

But now Ramalinga wanted to be the boss of the outfit he had co-founded. Within months there was friction among the Rajus and D.V.S. left in September 1992. In a peace deal brokered by the community elders, D.V.S. was given a hefty compensation but had to promise not to start a competing business for three years. After biding time as a consultant for three years, D.V.S. started a company called Visualsoft in 1995. Today, he runs the privately owned Gangavaram seaport in Vishakapatnam; Visualsoft has been long sold off. The easing out of D.V.S. is a good example of the Ramalinga style of operations, which he would demonstrate more effectively in the coming years. This involved using someone's expertise to build a business and then forcing him out to prevent him from becoming too powerful.

After D.V.S. Raju's exit, Ramalinga Raju's younger brother, Rama Raju, joined the company as managing director. But he, like his elder brother, was a zilch in technical matters. Then who would run the company? In came Srini Raju, an engineer from Regional Engineering College in Kurukshetra, who had a postgraduate degree from the US. More importantly, Srini and Ramalinga were married to sisters, making them brothers-in-law. Srini, who had earlier worked with Texas Instruments in the US and had also helped Satyam on a part-time basis, became the chief executive officer of Satyam. Srini drove the company for the next eight years before he himself was eased out.

In the next few years, Satyam took rapid strides and set up numerous subsidiaries and alliances. Satyam Infoway, a new company that became a name in the internet space, was established in late 1995 with its headquarters in Chennai. Hanuman Chowdhry, retired chairman of the Videsh Sanchar Nigam Limited, had by now joined the company's board. Before starting Satyam Infoway, Raju established a Satyam subsidiary called Satyam Enterprise Solutions. This was done in partnership with a foreign-owned consulting firm, Dun & Bradstreet.

Though Raju did not understand software, he was basking in the glory of the rapidly growing IT industry. At the initiative of Srini Raju, Satyam was readied for business opportunities that arose from the threat of Y2K, a bug that was feared would cause a global crash of computer systems on 1 January 2000. Satyam started a number of subsidiaries, mostly marketing ventures, including Satyam Japan in Tokyo, Satyam Asia in Singapore, and Satyam Europe, headquartered just outside London. For handling work specifically related to Y2K, a company called Dr Millennium was started. Satyam was going places.

Raju had not let go of Sri Satyam Spinning Mills, though its performance was not something to write home about. But to ensure that its poor showing would not cast a long shadow on Satyam Computer Services, the name of the mills was changed to Samrat Spinners. With the stock market going up in 1997, Raju went to the market for a public issue of Samrat Spinners for eighty lakh equity shares in order to raise Rs 8 crore. This done, Raju lost interest in the company and sold it to a local Hyderabad company in 1999. In 1998-99, the financial year before Raju sold off the company, Samrat Spinners had lost Rs 42.97 lakhs. Thus Raju was a failure as a textile industrialist.

Even as he exited, he dodged the APSIDC, which had given him Rs 50 lakh to start the venture. Neither did he pay any interest nor return any part of the principal. APSIDC kept writing letters to him, to which he responded by asking for more time. Raju had shown his true colours. If he could get away without paying back, he would.

Around this time, Raju felt that he should exploit the global financial markets as well. With technology being the big thing, the thought occurred to him that Satyam Infoway could be the vehicle for this. With the government relaxing norms for telecom and doing away with the monopoly of the

Videsh Sanchar Nigam, Satyam Infoway was doing well in the internet space and was the leading internet service provider (ISP) in the country. Raju planned to stage a coup, by listing a company directly on a foreign bourse even before it was part of the domestic stock exchange. Nasdaq, the upcoming stock exchange for technology shares in New York, was Raju's choice for listing the shares of Satyam Infoway. On 19 October 1999, the ADRs of Satyam Infoway were traded for the first time on Nasdaq and closed the day at $35 a share. This was nearly double the $18 per share price at which the issue was listed. Raju had succeeded in his plan – he was now truly part of the international circuit.

But the share had possibly not been listed on the Nasdaq by honest methods. The boy from Bhimavaram was alleged to have acted in an improper way and very soon a class action suit was filed against Satyam Infoway in the district courts of New York. The charges: Satyam Infoway had solicited and obtained excessive and undisclosed commissions for allocating shares to some investors. Moreover, it had allocated shares of Satyam Infoway to some collaborators in exchange for which they had promised to buy shares in the aftermarket at predetermined prices. In layman's terms, he had rigged the prices of the shares by paying large amounts of cash to some collaborators, who later used part of the cash to buy the shares at artificially high prices. They kept the rest of the cash as their commission for helping out Raju. All these were violations of the Securities Act of the US. The case is still being fought in the court.

Ramalinga Raju had tasted blood. Now he was in no mood to stop. Less than a year later, in July 2000, Satyam Infoway, in an all-share deal, bought a company called Indiaworld, which was portrayed as a leading worldwide online shopping mall. In effect, this company was nothing but a clutch of websites through which NRIs were sold mithais, garments, books and other items of interest to them. The cost of this acquisition worked out to $5 billion, and this is what caught the attention of analysts. They felt that this was a shady deal and that Raju had paid much more than was warranted to buy these websites. The speculation is that while Raju showed on paper that a huge amount had been paid, some of the money actually came back to him as kickbacks. Moreover, Raju had used money raised from the market through the IPO to buy Indiaworld.

What had the promoters done with the money? Had they paid back some of it to the Rajus as kickbacks? These were the questions that analysts sought to know. But Raju was not in a mood to stop. A few months down the line, Satyam Infoway bought another portal, Cricinfo.com, for a staggering Rs 1.7 billion. By this time, Raju's credibility in the investor community was seriously dented. Not surprisingly, the two acquisitions did not do well under Raju, and two years later, Satyam Infoway had to write off $1.2 billion from its books to account for losses.

Around this time, Ramalinga Raju decided that Satyam would have a fully owned subsidiary in the US. A company called Vision Compass Inc. was set up in 1999 in the US for the development, marketing and sale of specific software products. Till then, all software companies developed software as ordered by clients abroad. Raju felt that Satyam would take a step forward and make stand-alone products that he would market himself. But he failed woefully, and three years later, the company had to be wound up even as Satyam took a loss of Rs 125 crore on its books.

Even in the midst of all this, Raju's mind was working on raising more funds from the American bourses. This time he decided to list Satyam Computers on the NYSE. In May 2001, Satyam's ADR was listed on NYSE, and the company raised $140.8 million. Raju told investors that he was going to use the funds for strategic acquisitions, infrastructure development and for retiring previously raised debts. Acquisitions, Raju declared, were a better and faster of way of growing. What he did not say was that acquisitions also afforded a chance to indulge in accounting jugglery. In the event, there were no acquisitions by Raju in the aftermath of the ADR issue, but the legal expenses of his company rose sharply. This was explained away by saying that the cost of compliance was higher in the US and the rising lawyer costs were to ensure that proper systems were followed. But those in the know of things were not convinced that Satyam's legal expenses could double from Rs 27.5 crore to Rs 66.24 crore just for payments on this account abroad. It was felt that money was being siphoned off.

But those were heady days circa 2000. The feel-good factor was all around, and with the Indian market abounding with crooks, Raju's transgressions were forgotten. Around this time, Raju was befriended by Ketan Parekh, the biggest bull operator in the market after Harshad Mehta (who was imprisoned). Very soon, Satyam was one of the K-10 shares, that is, one of the ten favourite shares that the bull operator was fond of buying and pushing up on the Bombay Stock Exchange. Naturally, many shareholders of Satyam were making a killing by selling the shares, then buying them again, and then again selling them at a higher price. For ordinary shareholders, doing this was not illegal. But if Raju was ramping up share prices, then he was guilty of what is called 'insider trading' in technical parlance, that is, taking advantage of privileged insider information.

The lad who barely two decades ago had no clue about what to do in life had become a big name; the IT sector was booming in Hyderabad, and Chief Minister Chandrababu Naidu had decided to project Raju as the poster boy of the city. Industry recognition was also not lagging, and this came in the form of awards like the *Dataquest* Man of the Year, reflecting his new status.

Raju began to imagine that he was in the league of Azim Premji and N.R. Narayana Murthy and started taking himself more seriously than ever before. He also felt that the utility of Srini Raju was over. Persisting with him meant making him very important, and a stage could come in the future when Raju would not be in a position to outmanoeuvre him. But Srini Raju was too closely associated with Satyam (there was no way that he wouldn't have known about the alleged shady goings-on), and moreover, there was this angle of kinship. There would be tension at home if things went out of hand. All this implied that Srini Raju had to be rewarded very handsomely.

In pursuance of this idea, in mid-2000, Satyam Enterprise Solutions was merged with Satyam Computers in such a way as to benefit Srini Raju hugely. Before the merger, 800,000 shares of Satyam Enterprise Solutions were relinquished in favour of Srini Raju at Rs 10 per share. Then the two companies were merged with a swap ratio of 1:1. That meant that one share of Satyam Enterprise Solution entitled shareholders of the outfit to get one share of Satyam Computers. Thus Srini Raju got 800,000 shares of Satyam Computers at Rs 10 each. Considering that the market price of Satyam at the time was approximately Rs 1,900, this was a throwaway price. Srini had overnight minted a fortune.

When the news reached the market, there was anger amongst investors, but Raju was unmoved. The annual general meeting (AGM) was held the day after the news had broken out. In a remarkable display of nonchalance, Raju decided to skip the meeting.

By now, Raju had got the hang of the IT business and decided to take charge of the affairs of the company himself. A few years ago, the name of Satyam Constructions (a company started by

Raju in 1988, just a year after Satyam was floated, and handled by his brother Rama Raju) had been changed to Maytas (Satyam spelt in reverse), and this company had started to pick up.

It was around this time in 2001 that Raju (by his own confession) started falsifying the accounts of Satyam. In his arrogance, Raju thought that nobody would question him. This was especially so as he had become a mega IT icon who was close to Chief Minister Chandrababu Naidu. And the NDA government in New Delhi relied on Naidu's support. In fact, Raju's shenanigans caught the attention of the income tax department in 2002 and also that of the department of company affairs, which felt that there was something wrong somewhere about Satyam's accounting practices.

The persistence of a lone income tax deputy commissioner exposed the complicated tax evasion by Raju. It all began when the tax official found an unusually large number of Form 15 H applications filed by members of the Raju family. Under the tax laws, senior citizens in India are exempt from paying TDS (tax deduction at source) and what caught the lady officer's attention was that an amount of Rs 19.6 crore was shown as fixed deposits in the name of Raju's father, Satyanarayana, his mother, Appalanarasamma, and other elderly relatives. Obviously, no taxes had been paid on this. The officer investigated and found that the money had been diverted, through a complex web of transactions, from Satyam into the account of the senior members of the Raju family.

The lady persisted with her investigations, but was intimidated by Raju allegedly through his political influence. The officer was transferred and Raju escaped by paying taxes of about Rs 5 crore, though the entire amount of Rs 19.6 crore should have been confiscated. If Raju had been halted in his tracks then, the scam would not have grown to the dimensions that it did by 2009.

But why did Raju actually start fudging the accounts of Satyam, inflating the company's revenues and profits? Strange as it would seem, it was partly a deep inferiority complex that made Raju embark on this unholy path. Raju knew that he could neither match Narayana Murthy nor Azim Premji, as Satyam procured much of its business by quoting cheaper rates. Satyam's main strength was that the projects were executed reasonably well at low prices. But Andhraites had made him into an icon and he had to live up to this image. There was no way Raju could allow Satyam to show annual results that were vastly inferior to those of Infosys or Satyam. So began the process of cooking the books that ultimately led the man to prison.

Once Raju had embarked on this path, he possibly began to swindle his own company of its money (the latter is, however, yet to be proven conclusively by the law enforcement agencies). The fact that Satyam had been listed on the NYSE and had businesses in dozens of countries spread across North America, Europe and Asia made this task relatively easy. Different countries had different laws and different banks operated differently. Close observers say that Raju realized that he could exploit this diversity to his advantage and stash away funds that would never be discovered. And the fact that the IT business grew very rapidly over the next few years probably made Raju's job less complex. A lot of new clients in different geographical locations were being added and so were revenues.

But all the same, the process of fudging accounts of a company with revenues topping hundreds of crores is no joke. Raju needed the money for two reasons: one, to buy land, and secondly, to show impressive revenue figures, so that the company's share prices and market capitalization could get a boost. It is an elaborate exercise, more so if fudging and swindling are taking place simultaneously. With thousands of vouchers, bills and cheques, a huge infrastructure of dedicated staff is required for criminal activities. An additional requirement is that the staff involved in this shady activity should not talk about it either within the office or outside. Business managers also have to be kept insulated from the goings-on. Further, statutory auditors, who are required to go through the books of accounts of the company with a fine comb and certify the genuineness of the accounts, also have to be managed.

After thinking about it deeply – and this thought process went on for months – Raju decided he would have to establish a system where everything was compartmentalized. Information flow would be restricted and would be passed on strictly on a need-to-know basis. The end result was that a central accounts team was created, headed by Srinivasa Vadlamani, who was Raju's trusted aide and partner in crime. Vadlamani would be the nodal point for fudging: he would direct his team to change figures, create fictitious bills, vouchers and the works. This new team would also prepare the accounts of Satyam, but to insulate them from prying business managers, each business unit was provided with a finance unit. Managers of these finance units would only compile the revenues and costs of the units and pass them on to the central accounts team.

As the fudging increased, some business managers did suspect that something was amiss. Their suspicions were aroused by the fact that the final accounts of the company seemed to show a lower profitability of their business. On asking, they were told that their costs were actually higher than what they had compiled because some 'companywide' costs had been apportioned to them. These questions were rare because they were not encouraged, and the accountants of the fifteen-strong central team – a mix of professionals and family members – kept to themselves and behaved as if they were not answerable to anybody. For their role in the scam, Raju of course gave them handsome rewards in the form of Satyam's shares whose value was continually going up in the market.

With IT growing rapidly and Satyam getting business increasingly from international clients, Raju realized that it was time to get an image makeover for Satyam. Hitherto, Satyam was largely a Telugu company, and additionally, it had a large number of Rajus. Post-2000, Satyam was hiring thousands of new staff every year, the maximum intake being from engineering colleges in Andhra Pradesh. Raju felt he had to live up to local expectations and hire more people from the state.

However, this often led to unworthy hirings from not so reputed institutions in the districts. As a result, the quality of manpower of Satyam was falling. Discipline was also lax in the company. Raju knew all this but had turned a blind eye to it. It was not that no work was being done in Satyam, but the company's work ethic was fast turning into that of a sarkari company, where some work gets done, but its quality leaves a lot to be desired.

By 2004, Raju realized that this 'chalta hai' work ethic could go on no more. Quality concerns were being raised by clients and clearly there was a need for re-engineering the human resource. Since most of Satyam's clients were foreign, Raju decided to include some 'gora' managers in his company. In line with this, some foreign managers were hired to head key verticals like energy and insurance. Raju also conceived of the Satyam School of Learning and the Satyam School of Leadership and hired expats at exorbitant salaries to head them. These schools – as per Raju's plan – would be in-house training institutions to polish the talent that Satyam had and groom future leaders. And even if no leaders emerged from these learning schools, at least the corporate world at large would applaud Satyam's efforts.

Multicultural organizations were becoming fashionable, and so Raju hired interns from various countries for Satyam. It is a different matter that all of them left after working for sometime in the company's headquarters in Hyderabad.

In all these years, even as Satyam was growing in revenues, profits and stature, Raju was looking for an exit path. He knew that Satyam was not as awesome a company as it looked to the world. Of course, the company had its strengths, but with all the fudging it would soon go bust. Before it did so, Raju would have to exit. He could clean up the company and sell it; there would be certainly many buyers for Satyam. Raju had got overtures from IBM, but he was a tough bargainer. He kept the talks on without coming to a deal.

There was also another reason why Raju wanted to get out of Satyam: it was taking too much of his time. His first love was realty and land and that is where he wanted to be in these happening times. He could not leave the company to the care of his younger brother, Rama Raju, who was mediocre. His only claim to fame was his association with Ramalinga. The company could not be left in the hands of professionals: even if evidence of swindling could be hidden, all the falsification was bound to be exposed one day. The only top professional who was part of the scam was the vice-president of finance, Srinivasa Vadlamani. But he knew nothing of IT; he was just a chartered accountant who carried out Raju's orders. On his own he would be a disaster.

By 2005-06, Satyam was a company with revenues of a billion dollars and joined a select club of Indian IT companies. Satyam was now operating across all continents and had thousands of customers. This included many Fortune 500 companies as well. Raju continued to ape the ways of Infosys and Wipro, and like them, tried to be a one-stop shop for outsourcing. He set up a BPO company called Nipuna as a subsidiary of Satyam but later converted it into Satyam BPO to leverage on the Satyam brand name.

Buying companies to ramp up the strength of Satyam and also to expand his business empire still continued to be Raju's passion, and in line with this, in April 2005, he bought CitiSoft Inc. a UK-based consulting firm with operations in investment management. The price paid was $38 million. Two months later, he bought the Singapore-based Knowledge Dynamics, a consulting solutions provider, at a price of $3.3 million. In October 2007, Raju bought Nitor Global Solutions, a UK-based infrastructure management service and consultancy group, for $5.5 million. In January 2008, a Chicago-based consultancy firm, Bridge Strategy Group, was picked up, and three months later, Caterpillar Inc's market research and customer analytics operation were bought for $95.5 million. Satyam also listed itself on a stock exchange, ADS Next, in the Netherlands. This listing would allow the company to raise more money.

To keep up with the Joneses, Raju was now misrepresenting figures more furiously than ever before. By the middle of 2008, Satyam had become a $2 billion company. The company was getting prestigious contracts too, including one for developing software for FIFA's World Cup for 2010 and 2014. Raju was also being offered high positions such as that of the vice-president of Nasscom, and honours such as Corporate Citizen of the Year, Entrepreneur of the Year, and the Golden Peacock Award for Best Corporate Governance (for 2007).

But experts had a hunch that everything was not right in his company, and IT analysts disputed Satyam's status as the fourth-largest IT company in India after Tata Consultancy Services, Infosys and Wipro. Tech magazines like *Dataquest* placed it at number six, behind IBM and Hewlett Packard.

Though Raju batted with a straight bat in public, he was getting increasingly wary about Satyam. The company was now fast spinning out of his control. Legal suits were also coming up thick and fast. Some of them were not mere disputes about interpretations of contracts but involved charges of fraud.

A good example was that of Upaid, a privately owned telecom company registered in the British Virgin Islands. Satyam Enterprise Solutions had executed a project for developing software for its mobile prepaid technology. As is the practice in the industry, after the work was done, Upaid went to register the patent for this technology. Imagine its shock when it found that two other telecom companies, Qualcomm and Verizon, were already using this technology. Either Satyam or some of its engineers had sold off the technology to Qualcomm or Verizon after doing the work at Upaid's expense. Upaid filed a $1 billion suit in Texas; the case was still on when Raju confessed.

By the beginning of 2008, things were so chaotic in Satyam that nobody, not even Raju, knew how many people were employed in his empire. For the record, Satyam claimed that it had some 53,000 employees. But there was a lot of double counting. There were provident fund accounts for only a little more than 43,622 employees. Additionally, around 1,500 employees were working for overseas subsidiaries. That would make the total headcount of Satyam 45,000 at the most. A large number of employees – no one knew how many – were on the bench, without work but on the company rolls. Even the HRD department was clueless.

Whatever be the actual number of employees in Satyam, one thing was clear: the information systems were very poor. Transparency was at a discount and opaqueness was the order of the day. But that's what suited Raju the most.

FIVE

The Realty Show

On 17 December 1998, Chandrababu Naidu went to
Bangalore and did what no other chief minister of
Andhra Pradesh had done before. Calling a meeting of top local
industrialists at Hotel Taj Westend, he invited them to set up
shop in Andhra Pradesh. 'You will find us very friendly, helpful
and ever ready to go the extra mile to help you set up your
units,' Chandrababu said. Naidu's was a pleading style, and for
corporates in Bangalore, who were then at the receiving end of
an indifferent Karnataka chief minister, J.H. Patel, this came as
a breath of fresh air.

Soon, industrialists from Bangalore were making a beeline
to Naidu's chief ministerial office in Hyderabad with project
proposals. So warmly were they received that these honchos
had no hesitation in recommending the Andhra Pradesh chief
minister to their friends in other parts of the country. In a short
while, Hyderabad became the destination for businessmen.
Apart from wooing state industrialists, Naidu was also building

relations with local businessmen. This was necessary, Naidu's spin doctors had told him, for his fair name to spread fast.

One of the corporate bigwigs whom Naidu assiduously cultivated was Ramalinga Raju. The Satyam promoter's quiet confidence and go-getting abilities impressed Naidu, who realized that this educated entrepreneur could well become the mascot of Andhra Pradesh. The two spent a considerable amount of time together and came to the conclusion that a mere welcoming attitude would not get investments into the state: to achieve this, the 400-year-old laidback city of Hyderabad would have to be transformed, and this visible change would have to be showcased. This was an almost impossible job considering that the old city of Hyderabad was a maze of dirty, narrow lanes. Transforming the city was an exercise that would take ten years, but if Hyderabad had to be showcased, then quick results had to be demonstrated.

Thus came the idea of a spanking new city that was a part of Hyderabad and yet not quite so. Cyberabad was a result of this branding exercise and this city – as its name denoted – was conceptualized as a hub for the hi-tech industry. Land was quickly acquired in the picturesque and rocky highland villages around Hyderabad. A Hi Tech City soon became a reality. Satyam also put up buildings in this enclave, even as the fame of Hyderabad quickly spread far and wide. So much so that on a visit to India in 2000, US President Bill Clinton decided to stop over at Hyderabad.

Chandrababu Naidu realized that this was his chance to catapult himself to the global stage. He decided to enlist Ramalinga Raju's support for this purpose. It suited both: while Naidu wanted to woo business, Raju wanted to be close to politicians in power. As a result, Raju shared the dais with Clinton and Naidu when a limited-audience public show was organized for the visiting US president. This was Raju's introduction to the world at large. Even as he sat on the dais, doyens of Indian industry such as Ratan Tata and even local bosses with clout such as Ramoji Rao of the Eenadu group, were down below. Raju had arrived and had become the cynosure of all eyes – although everybody complained about the long and boring speech that he subjected the audience to.

Post Clinton, Naidu continued with his plans to develop Hyderabad, and as Cyberabad grew at a rapid pace, so did Raju. Satyam also benefited in this boom period as Indian IT was able to make a mark in the US and western European markets. Within a short period of time, Ramalinga Raju and Satyam became household names in India, the latter one of the preferred destinations for students passing out of engineering colleges and a favoured scouting place for parents seeking matches for their daughters.

In the election of 2004, much against public expectation, Chandrababu Naidu was routed. Political analysts suggested that with his focus on Hyderabad and IT, he had forgotten all about the farmers and the countryside and that it was these rural areas that punished him. The Congress, led by Rajasekhara Reddy, strode to power on the promise of seven hours of free electricity to farmers. Raju was dismayed: there would be no focus on the development of Hyderabad and IT, he thought. What worried him most was that Rajasekhara Reddy, popularly known as YSR, was reputed to be a vindictive man. He was a friend of friends and enemy of enemies. He would not take very kindly to Naidu's favourites and friends.

Raju's apprehensions were not wrong. YSR started giving short shrift to all Naidu favourites. But at the same time, Raju was pleasantly surprised when he saw that like Naidu, YSR was also interested in the development of Hyderabad and its infrastructure. This was contrary to YSR's image, elected as he had been on the rural plank. In fact, it soon became clear that the new chief minister wanted to go full steam ahead with his own plans to build the infrastructure of Hyderabad and indeed, the entire state of Andhra Pradesh. Raju realized that he had to be friends with the new boss of the state. It was not an easy job, but ultimately Raju managed to befriend YSR and get into his good books.

Though Raju had become famous as a successful IT entrepreneur, his interest lay elsewhere. He fancied himself as a construction baron. This was not surprising because he had grown up in a family whose business had much to do with land. His father, Satyanarayana Raju, was a big farmer who had himself set up a small construction business. In the mid-1960s, the entire family, led by Satyanarayana, had migrated to Hyderabad. Satyanarayana had set up an enclave for the Raju clan in Medchal, then on the outskirts of Hyderabad, and had started buying land in the region. Ramalinga Raju himself had set up a construction company called Satyam Constructions Private Limited in May 1988, barely a year after he launched Satyam Computer Services. Five years later, in July 1993, this company became a deemed public limited company.

Ten years to the day after it was founded, Satyam Construction's name was changed to Maytas Infra Limited. This name change had to do with the rapid growth of Satyam Computers: Raju did not want people to confuse one company with the other. At the same time, the appellation of Infra was also a reflection of the changing nature of the construction industry – from development of realty and housing, it was now fast becoming a business of infrastructure development.

By the time Rajasekhara Reddy came to power, Maytas was already progressing well. It was executing a few road and power projects, and Raju was in possession of quite a bit of land. Following in the footsteps of his father, Ramalinga had started buying land in a big way since 1999, which was around the time that he became close to Naidu. To circumvent the land ceiling acts in Andhra Pradesh, Raju had spawned unlisted companies to buy up land.

In total, Raju had incorporated 327 companies to deal in 'agriculture and allied activities', a euphemism for the sale and purchase of land. These companies had exotic names ranging from Vamsadhara Agro to Bharani Agro, and from Anuradha Agri Tech to Dhanistha Agro. There was no pattern to the names: some were named after stars and constellations, others after rivers. All the companies were not floated in the name of Raju. Eighty-three of these land-purchasing companies were in the names of Ramalinga, his wife, Nandini, and their two sons, Teja and Rama Raju (junior). Seventy-eight companies were in the names of his middle brother Suryanarayana, his wife, Jhansi, and their children, Purnima and Satyanarayana Raju (junior). Another eighty-six companies were in the names of his youngest brother, Rama Raju, his wife, Radha, and their children, Deepti and Rahul. There were eighty other companies floated in the names of Raju's distant relatives and trusted employees. Not surprisingly, the 'offices' of all the 327 companies were located across twelve addresses, all in Hyderabad.

Buying land in different names had another advantage: nobody knew how much land he had gobbled up in and around Hyderabad. Raju got the moral courage to buy land because Andhra Pradesh is a feudal state where the land ceiling acts are nearly always observed in the breach. There were many other top businessmen who had bought land around Hyderabad, but their holdings were minuscule compared to Raju's.

The speed at which Rajasekhara Reddy moved on the development agenda created a boom in the realty scene in Hyderabad. Though a chip off the old Congress block, Rajasekhara Reddy had his own way of looking at things. He realized that the perpetually empty state exchequer could be boosted if the state government itself became an active participant in the realty business. Soon enough, Reddy's government was developing land and auctioning it. Much of this land was government land that was lying fallow. It also included disputed land. There was a large tract of Wakf land around Hyderabad that had been given out for charity by the erstwhile Nizams of Hyderabad. This was now controlled by the state government and Rajasekhara Reddy started auctioning this land too.

These moves, coupled with the fact that there was a real estate boom across the nation, boosted land and property prices in Hyderabad between 2004 and 2007. By a conservative estimate, the year on year escalation on property prices in Hyderabad was over 30 per cent, and in these three years, real estate prices doubled. Raju tasted blood and went for the kill, purchasing more and more land, as a contractor raj seemed to prevail in Hyderabad..

But Raju was not buying land at random, he was doing so with a plan. 'Raju's modus operandi was to buy a few pieces of land in a particular area at a price much higher than that prevailing in the market. This would create a higher benchmark in the area and was tantamount to rigging of prices,' says a player in the Hyderabad real estate market. The most glaring example of this was in the auction of over five acres of land next to the K.B.R. Park – notified as a national park, it serves as the green lungs for Hyderabad – in the posh Jubilee Hill area. Though the prevailing price was between Rs 50,000-60,000 per square yard, the Rajus bid a staggering Rs 120,000 per square yard and clinched the deal. 'When I asked Rama Raju with whom we had done business in the past, he said "What to do? Our partners in this business insisted on bidding this high." But he was clearly fibbing,' recollects a leading realtor of the city.

There were other ways too in which Raju's men pushed prices up. 'I also buy land. And I remember that when I went to prospect land in an area two years ago, the land dealers – who were obviously Raju's men – directed me to another area. They said Raju was buying land there. Prices will quickly escalate and you may find it profitable to buy there,' says a steel mill owner who invests in land.

Some other property players assert that at least some of Raju's agents specialized in buying land that was under dispute. The price for such land was cheaper but purchasing it reflected Raju's confidence that he would be able to clear the land of all encumbrances. Hyderabad also has a lot of 'assigned' land in its outer reaches which is meant to be distributed to the landless. Trade in such land is prohibited by law, but the market buzz is that the Rajus thought nothing of picking up such land. However, in this Raju's men were not alone: many other realtors did the same.

Buying land and pushing their prices up was not the end of the game, and Raju realized that money was really to be made in property development. In this Raju was greatly inspired by the example of DLF Ltd. He admired the way K.P. Singh had convinced farmers in Gurgaon to part with their land, and felt awed by the way DLF launched housing schemes using its clout in the government. Thus the company was virtually responsible for catapulting this small town in Haryana on the high road to prosperity. Raju wanted to do another Gurgaon on the outskirts of Hyderabad.

But another Gurgaon could be created only through a proper corporate mechanism which would also have access to huge funds. It is in pursuance of this idea that Raju set up Maytas Properties in 2005 as a privately owned company. For starters, Maytas Properties began its activities in Hyderabad, where Raju already owned a considerable amount of land. With the real estate market booming and many NRIs from Andhra Pradesh seeking property back home, Raju figured that high-end residential projects and townships would make good business sense.

The Maytas Hill County project, spread across 300 acres in the Bachupally area of Hyderabad and with state-of-the-art facilities, was conceived as a result of this thinking. Flats and villas in Maytas Hill County would cost between Rs 40 lakhs and Rs 3.5 crore. Raju wanted to pioneer new concepts for India, and with special economic zones (SEZs) being created everywhere, the concept of 'walk to work' was mooted by him. He visualized IT parks coming up in the vicinity of Maytas Hills County, and people who worked there could walk home to his housing complex. Raju proposed setting up three SEZs and the proposal was quickly cleared by the government. The projects are still in the works but are unlikely to be completed in the aftermath of Raju's confession. In fact, Maytas now wants to get out of two of the SEZ projects.

But that was not all Ramalinga was planning. In association with ICICI, he bid for 5.7 acres of premium land adjacent to K.B.R. Park. Raju proposed to develop 1,000,000 square feet of space in this land, including a five-star hotel, luxury apartments, and high-end retail space. Close by, he wanted to develop 70,000 square feet of space for IT offices and residences that would overlook the verdant K.B.R. Park.

These grandiose plans required money and while Raju was mobilizing finances on his own from private sources, he also tied up with big funds other than the usual banks and financial institutions. He entered into an agreement with Infinite India Investment Management Company, one of the country's largest investment firms focussed on real estate. This company was partly owned by J.M. Financial of Mumbai, which was one of the leading financial services group in India, and partly owned by a US private equity firm called SRS. Infinite India invested a staggering Rs 600 crore in Maytas Properties in the form of convertible debentures that would be later converted into equity. The money, as per the agreement, was to be used for implementing the upcoming projects of Maytas Properties and also for land acquisition for new projects in Chennai, Bangalore, Nagpur, Vijayawada, Vishakapatnam and Cochin. Ramalinga Raju was also proposing a public issue for the company, so that even more funds could be raised for faster growth.

As the real estate market became more attractive, Raju started devoting more time to the affairs of Maytas Properties and began spending hours together at the office of the company that was also located in Hyderabad's Hi Tech City, not too far away from the Satyam corporate headquarters.

While building and planning for Maytas Properties, Ramalinga Raju was not oblivious of his family and paternal responsibilities. As a loving father to his second son, he also wanted to bequeath a lasting gift to him. Thus Rama Raju (junior) was made the vice chairman of Maytas Properties, and 50 per cent of the shareholding of the company was vested in his name.

Raju was not focussed on Maytas Properties alone. Though he rarely went to the office of Maytas Infra, which was located in Hyderabad's Begumpet area right opposite the chief minister's official residence, Raju wanted to build this company as a gift to his elder son, Teja Raju. He was inducted into Maytas Infra in 2001 but Ramalinga wanted Teja to direct the company. However, there was a problem: a significant part of the shares of Maytas Infra were in the name of Ramalinga's brothers Suryanarayana and Rama Raju (senior). Collectively, the two along with their spouses held 20 per cent of Maytas Infra. In contrast, Teja owned virtually nothing in the company. It would not be easy to make the two brothers give up their stakes in the company.

Even as Ramalinga was mulling over how to bequeath Maytas Infra to his elder son, business was growing by leaps and bounds. The country – especially Andhra Pradesh – was in the midst of a construction boom, and Raju, with closer proximity now to the powers that be than before, succeeded in garnering a huge volume of business. This included contracts for building irrigation projects and construction of roads, including highways.

With airport modernization going apace in the country, Maytas also successfully bid to win a contract to modernize and take over the operation of Gulbarga and Shimoga airports in Karnataka in partnership with Vienna International Airport Company and another Hyderabad company, Nagarjuna Construction. It also successfully bid for constructing and then running a three-million-ton-per-annum deep water seaport on the coast of Andhra Pradesh at a cost of Rs 1,650 crore. Maytas secured diverse orders for construction, ranging from building townships in Jammu and Kashmir and erecting malls in Lucknow to building storage facilities for Reliance at Jamnagar and residential complexes in Kerala, Kanpur and Chennai, besides a Singapore-class township in Hyderabad. Road projects included work relating to the Mumbai–Pune expressway and a road corridor between Bangalore and Mysore.

Under Raju's leadership, Maytas Infra also won dozens of contracts for irrigation work across the country, most of them in Andhra Pradesh. Irrigation projects being a priority of the Rajasekhara Reddy government, Maytas was straightaway given a 'mobilization amount' by the government, a sort of advance to start work. This meant that even before the projects were implemented, the cash registers of Maytas had begun ringing.

'Go and get more orders. Let our order books swell,' were Raju's instructions to his managers. Raju intended to execute the projects – but in his own sweet time. Raju's men depended much on their relationship with government bodies and agencies to secure land orders, and to further ensure that they secured contracts, Maytas bid low. This was a sure-shot way of getting competitors out of the way.

Other plans had also been devised by an ambitious Raju. One was to enter into numerous joint ventures and partnerships with other companies. In line with this, virtually for every project that Maytas secured, a joint venture association was formed. That way Raju was able to co-opt other ambitious contractors, who would otherwise be his competitors, into his scheme of things. There was another advantage in this for Raju: when he presented the books of Maytas along with the actual financial position, he would be able to show inflated figures. That the figures would reflect the financials of the joint venture companies in which Maytas would only be holding minority stake would facilitate such fudging. It may not have been morally proper to use those figures to boost the financial statements of Maytas, but Raju had sought the help of some consulting firms who said that there was nothing illegal in doing so.

Soon enough, Maytas acquired a larger-than-life image. To outside observers Maytas looked a far bigger and more attractive company than it actually was. By the time Raju went under, Maytas had seven joint ventures and eleven associate companies. The ventures had names as diverse as Maytas-Shankarnarayana, NCC-Maytas Pocharam company, Cyberabad Expressways Private Limited, Brindavan Infra Company Limited and K.V. Nilachal Power Private Limited. A few months before Raju confessed, when the slowdown had not yet set in, Teja Raju was telling shareholders of the company the 'macroeconomic environment augments the prospects for Maytas. The increase in infrastructure investment from 5 per cent of the GDP to 9 per cent in 2007-12 augurs well for us. The massive investment of US $494 billion proposed in the infrastructure sector promises a lot of business for us.'

Raju also wanted Maytas to do business abroad. He established a company called Dhabi Maytas Contracting Company to execute projects in Abu Dhabi. Maytas also floated two other overseas companies: Maytas (Singapore) Holding Pvt Ltd and Infrastrade FZE. The former was a shell company created just to hold investments of Maytas in subsidiaries and joint venture companies. The latter was incorporated in Ras Al Khaimah free trade zone in the United Arab Emirates, the purpose being to trade in building and construction materials. Through this company Raju hoped to procure materials cheaply to be used in buildings in India.

But Raju's sights were not limited to the Gulf area or South East Asia. He established a company called Maytas Mineral Resources Limited as a subsidiary of Maytas to prospect for coal, iron and copper ore in far-off lands that included South Africa, Australia and even Latin American countries. 'There are no limits to growth because there are no limits to the human capacity for intelligence, imagination and achievements,' Raju told his colleagues while setting the mission statement for the company.

Even though Raju managed to get more and more orders for Maytas Infra, the company did not have a particularly great name, at least in Andhra Pradesh, when it came to reliability in project execution. Numerous divisional engineers of the irrigation department overseeing projects being executed by Maytas were upset with the way the company went about its work. But their complaint with higher authorities went unheeded, so close were the connections of Maytas Infra with the powers that be. In fact, in some cases, engineers who dared complain were transferred to other positions.

In construction circles, Maytas's reputation was that of a company more interested in filling its order books than implementing the projects. Brokers who dealt with Maytas's share in the market also felt that the undue dependence on the government for grant of projects was a distinct risk for the company. 'There could be political pressures, there could be financial pressures....What would happen if the government were to slow down on outlays for infrastructure projects? That would hit the order book of Maytas,' wrote an analyst in his report about the company.

Even auditors were not entirely happy with the way Maytas operated. 'The scope and coverage of the internal audit system requires to be enlarged to be commensurate with the size and nature of its business,' the company's statutory auditor reported while going through the company's financials for 2006-07. Since auditors, by nature, are conservative about what they write, this essentially meant that there was the possibility of chicanery taking place. A year later, the auditors examining the financials for 2007-08 had to offer the same comment. Nothing had changed in Maytas – the management was not interested in tightening controls in the company that was expanding rapidly. The auditors also found that Maytas had given loans worth nearly Rs 64 crore to nineteen companies without insisting on any collateral (this money is believed to have been siphoned off to the private companies run by the Raju family).

With the equity market on a steep upward curve, Ramalinga Raju was not a person to let the opportunity to net resources from the market pass by. By the beginning of 2007, he was planning a public issue for Maytas Infra that would catapult it to even greater heights. Raju also saw this as the opportune

moment to restructure the equity of Maytas Infra to put Teja
Raju in a commanding position.

As part of the plan, Teja Raju was named promoter of Maytas
Infra. But there were two other co-promoters as well: these
were not individuals but corporate bodies – SNR Investments
and Veeyes Investments. Both these companies had been set up
in 2004 with the express purpose of carrying out business in
portfolio investments. Interestingly, SNR Investments was also
promoted by Teja, who held nearly 50 per cent of the equity
of the company. Veeyes Investments was half owned by Teja,
the other part under the control of Jhansi Rani, the wife of
Suryanarayana Raju.

Raju's mind worked in a complicated fashion and seldom
did he take a straight path. In line with this, forty-one other
companies were also named as part promoters of Maytas Infra.
These were part of the 327 privately held companies spawned by
Raju to trade in land. In addition to making Teja the promoter
of Maytas Infra, Raju also named a promoter group for the
company. This included his wife Nandini, Teja, Teja's wife Divya,
and their minor daughter, Anjali, besides himself.

What is interesting is that Ramalinga's brothers, Suryanarayana
and Rama, who had been directors of the company since
its inception, exited the board within a span of two months
of Teja's induction as promoter of the company. They were
greatly disappointed because they were being pushed out at
a time when Maytas was growing very rapidly. But they could
hardly complain because Ramalinga Raju was responsible for
establishing and zealously pushing forward the empire. The two
at best had a supportive role: their careers depended on elder
brother being around. This was especially true of Suryanarayana,
who had barely passed out of high school. Further, they came
from a family where the tradition was to respect elders at all

costs. No sibling or son uttered anything in opposition to the elder brother or father.

Though brokers saw the risk in investing in Maytas for its excessive dependence on government projects, they assessed Raju and realized that he was a safe horse to back as far as the public issue of the company was concerned. 'Maytas has extensive experience and strong track record in construction business. It has a diversified portfolio across infrastructural sectors and geographical locations. It is an integrated player with in-house managerial abilities,' the brokers declared, assessing the initial public issue (IPO) in September 2007. And coupled with the boom time in which it was operating, the public issue of Maytas was a roaring success. The issue was oversubscribed by a staggering sixty-seven times, though a lot of Raju's family members had bought shares to shore it up.

With his dual character and split personality, if Raju could break laws and norms with impunity, he could also do good for society, or at least pose to do so. In July 2001, shortly after his father passed away, Ramalinga thought that about doing something meaningful for society in the memory of his father. Thus was born the Byrraju Foundation, with he and his two brothers as the trustees. Needless to add, Ramalinga was the moving spirit – like in his business – and the other two were just marking their presence. Raju was interested in the upliftment of villages in Andhra Pradesh, and more specifically in his home district of Godavari. He had himself spent his childhood in this district and had gone to school up to class VII in a village. Moreover, a large Raju clan lived in the area.

The foundation – supported continually by Raju, who often dropped into its office – was in a short time able to establish programmes for health, education, water supply, livelihood training, sanitation and the like. As an example, the foundation

Before the bubble burst:
Ramalinga Raju at home, surrounded by his books.

Ramalinga Raju's residence in the upmarket
Jubilee Hill area of Hyderabad.

TV vans gather outside the Satyam headquarters in Hyderabad's
Hi Tech City after news of Raju's confession broke.

Mediapersons crowd around Raju's car as he is brought to the
Nampally court a few days after his arrest in January 2009.

Onlookers and media outside Chanchalguda jail in Hyderabad,
where Raju was lodged.

Raju coming out of the Nampally criminal court.

In happier days: Raju with the finance minister, Pranab Mukherjee,
and former Britannia managing director, Sunil Alagh,
at a function in Hyderabad in 2008.

Raju getting an honorary PhD from Andhra University in Vizag in late
2007. Looking on is K. Rosaiah, who took over as chief minister of
Andhra Pradesh after the death of Y.S.R. Reddy in September 2009.

Raju with the late Andhra Pradesh chief minister, Y.S.R. Reddy, shortly after the latter began his term in 2004.

Raju with (from left) Ram Mynampati, Satyam president, Srinivas Vadlamani, chief financial officer, and T. Hari, chief of human resources, at a press conference to declare Satyam's annual results in April 2007 in Hyderabad.

Raju with the Telugu cinema superstar Chiranjeevi at the wedding
of the daughter of his brother, Rama, in Hyderabad.

Rama Raju and his wife with Chiranjeevi at their daughter's wedding.

Raju's wife, Nandini, with Bhuvaneswari, wife of the former Andhra Pradesh chief minister, Chandrababu Naidu.

Raju's sons Teja (left) and Rama (Jr) (right) with their respective wives.

Kingshuk Nag

The Rajus' ambitious real estate development project in Hyderabad, Maytas Hill County, involving high-end housing, is now on the rocks.

Kingshuk Nag

The Satyam Enclave, a residential complex mainly inhabited by the Raju community in the Medchal area of Hyderabad.

Raju set up the Emergency Management Research Institute, which pioneered the concept of ambulance on call.

The Byraaju Foundation, set up by Raju to take up developmental work for the Raju community.

The state-of-the-art Satyam Technology Centre, which stands on a huge tract of freehold land.

Satyam employees expressing their solidarity with their company by stamping their hands on a board outside the company office.

set up 200 health centres in 200 villages in six districts of Andhra Pradesh, which was visited by a physician once a day and had a full-time health worker. Medicines were also dispensed at subsidized rates from these health centres. In another instance, the foundation adopted 260 government schools in Andhra Pradesh's villages and selectively intervened to operate spoken English classes or introduce children to computers. Livelihood trainings – for trades like construction work, tailoring, fabric painting, etc – were imparted for a small fee. Raju's efforts were lauded and got the foundation many awards. This included the Federation of Indian Chambers of Commerce and Industry (FICCI) award for best corporate social responsibility, an IBM award for innovative rural education, an award for being a social catalyst, and for being the best NGO in the conservation of water.

But this was not the only social work that Raju did. He also began the Emergency Management and Research Institute (EMRI), which was a pioneering effort in emergency management services. Although impressive at first and well-intended, EMRI suffered from the Raju style of corporate governance. EMRI, which began its operations in Andhra Pradesh but is now present in many states like Gujarat, Uttarakhand, Goa, Rajasthan and Chennai city, operates a fleet of ambulances. In case of an emergency – a medical emergency or an emergency related to an accident or an attack by assailants – the person seeking help just has to dial 108. Within minutes an ambulance will arrive on the scene and ferry the person to a hospital.

Raju began this service with financial assistance from the state governments, bearing merely 5 per cent of the total cost. Many were impressed by EMRI, and so successful was it that the former president of India, A.P.J. Abdul Kalam, agreed to be the chairman of its board. Also on the board were CII mentor Tarun

Das and former Nasscom chief Kiran Karnik, who were to be later appointed on the Satyam board as government nominees after Raju confessed.

In the aftermath of Raju's departure, when new partners were sought to fund and run EMRI, a virtual Pandora's box opened up. These prospective partners discovered that there were a lot of grey areas in the way EMRI functioned. Even basic things like asset registers (which keep an inventory of the assets that an organization has) were not maintained. And neither was there any transparency in the way that vendors were chosen to supply medicines and other articles, despite it being an organization that had 1,600 ambulances and 13,000 employees. The supply chain management, including purchases and stores for such a huge organization, had never been audited. What was worse, a trustee by the name of Krishnam Raju controlled the educational trust on whose land EMRI stood. A company belonging to Krishnam Raju's son was undertaking major construction and civil works for EMRI, making the whole operation very fuzzy. In other words, the 'Midas touch' of Ramalinga Raju had pervaded EMRI as well.

Six

Derailed by a Rail Deal

Though he did not realize it then, Raju's downfall began the day he was awarded the metro rail project for Hyderabad. Focussed as he was on land and realty, Raju had never thought of bidding for the metro rail project till somebody explained to him the wonderful opportunity it presented a top entrepreneur like him.

The man who talked him into the project was the then vice-president of CII's Hyderabad chapter, Harishchandra Prasad. This was sometime in April 2008, when Prasad, who ran his own power company, Malaxmi Hydro, wondered if he could bid for the project. Realizing that he was too small an entrepreneur to enter the fray, he discussed the idea with his cousin, Trivikrama, who ran the upcoming Navbharat Group in the field of infrastructure. The cousin was interested, but his business was also not large enough to qualify him as a bidder for the project. It was at this point that Harishchandra and Trivikrama decided to approach a big baron like Raju as a partner. Prasad knew Raju quite well, so getting an appointment was not a problem.

When the two met Raju and broached the subject with him, the IT man was plainly all ears. 'That's a great idea. But Satyam can't do this business. Let's get Maytas into this,' Raju said. He also added: 'I am interested in involving my son Teja. Just ensure that he has some role in this project.'

That's how Raju entered the project that ultimately led to his downfall. Typically, as soon as the project was awarded to him, he ensured that Harishchandra Prasad was out of it. But more of that later. First, a look at why Hyderabad needed the metro rail and how this project was different from those in Kolkata and Delhi.

The foundations of Hyderabad were laid over four hundred years ago, in 1591, but it was only after Aurangzeb captured the fort of Golconda in 1687, in what was a culmination of a protracted war lasting twenty-five years, that the city started coming into prominence. The Nizams, who ruled Hyderabad for over 250 years, started off as Mughal governors of the Deccan, but as soon as the empire in Delhi started disintegrating, they declared themselves independent. Hyderabad city was the seat of the Nizams' power, and with their fabled wealth (they owned the Golconda mines from where diamonds such as the Kohinoor had been mined), they went about earnestly planning their capital city. Though considerable thought went into laying out gardens and erecting public buildings, the streets were, not surprisingly, very narrow. It was on this foundation that Hyderabad had continued to grow into the twentieth century. When Hyderabad became the capital of the new state of Andhra Pradesh in 1956, there was no attempt to rebuild the city.

It was only in 2000 that Chandrababu Naidu began the process of building the new city of Cyberabad, which would be adjacent to Hyderabad and also part of it. Though a huge area had been labelled Cyberabad, by the time Naidu demitted office, only a small part of the Hi Tech City had been readied. Disastrously, however, the roads even in this new city of Cyberabad had a width of no more than forty feet. The ill-effects of this began to be felt in two years' time. By 2005, Hyderabad was seeing frenetic construction, but the streets around which this activity was taking place were still narrow. It was at this time that the idea of a metro rail was conceived for Hyderabad.

But there was a catch: Hyderabad was perched atop the granite rocks of the Deccan plateau. This implied that digging deep in Hyderabad was a difficult job and an underground metro a near-impossibility. So the metro rail in Hyderabad would have to be totally different from the country's first metro in Kolkata, where the soft alluvial soil had made construction of an underground metro an easier proposition. Hyderabad's proposed metro system could also not be like that of Delhi, where the metro was partly below the ground and partly above. But how does one build a fully overground metro in a congested city? The only way to do it is by demolishing buildings, gardens and busy marketplaces. Civil society activists realized this and thus there was significant public opinion against the metro rail for Hyderabad. In fact, this is why Chandrababu Naidu did not plan for a metro seriously in his time, although the then minister of state for railways in the NDA government, Bandaru Dattatreya, who represented Secunderabad in the Lok Sabha, was keen on the idea. Instead, the Naidu regime favoured a multi-modal transport system (MMTS) that basically meant running special trains across the city on the existing rail system – much like in Mumbai.

The MMTS, a joint venture of the Hyderabad municipal corporation and the South Central Railway, started its operation on 9 August 2003 with two lines. The first line of twenty-eight kilometres ran from Secunderabad station to Lingapally, while the second line of fifteen kilometres operated from Secunderabad station to Faluknama. The project cost was merely $37 million, or Rs 178 crore. With fares ranging between Rs 3 and Rs 10, the MMTS, which ran eighty-four services a day and covered twenty-seven stations, became a quick success.

But once the Rajasekhara Reddy government took over in 2004, saboteurs quickly appeared from nowhere. The success of a suburban train system in a city like Hyderabad depends on bus connections from train stations. By December 2005 – when lobbying by vested interests for a metro rail system was in full swing – authorities started withdrawing bus services from suburban rail stations, asserting that these services were not viable. As a result, fewer commuters began to travel by rail, and the traffic fell. The authorities began to cut back on train services as well. This was a pity because to many commuters – especially those who worked in IT companies in the Hi Tech City – it was a fast and dependable means of travel from their homes to office and vice versa. Faced with the authorities' disinterest in MMTS, the commuters grouped into an association to take up the issue.

But the Reddy government ignored public opinion and seemed hell-bent on the metro rail project. It did not seem concerned that major landmarks of the city would have to be demolished to make way for the project. Egged on by the real estate lobby – of which Ramalinga Raju was a very active member (although he operated from the sidelines and was not yet a part of the metro rail lobby) – a team was set up to draw up a tentative route map for the metro rail. Three routes – aggregating sixty-five kilometres – were quickly chosen, and these ran from Miyapur to Lal Bahadur Shastri Nagar, from the Jubilee Bus Stand to Faluknama, and from Nagole to Shilparaman.

Without doing proper traffic studies, much less a feasibility report, the Andhra Pradesh government decided to have an elevated metro rail system for Hyderabad. There would be two lines on each of the routes – one for up traffic and the other for down traffic – and these lines would come up on a deck to be erected on the central meridian of the road.

Getting an in-principle approval from the Government of India was not a problem, what with the same Congress-led political formation holding power both in New Delhi and Hyderabad. Thus, one of the largest metro rail projects in the world in a public–private participation mode was cleared by the central government in 2008. The total cost was pegged at Rs 7,986 crore in 2006 (in two years this went up to Rs 12,212 crore). The first metro rail service would be rolled out in 2012. More importantly, as part of the approval it was decided to pre-qualify contractors who would later bid for the project to implement it on a build-operate-transfer (BOT) basis. (Under the BOT scheme, the contractor would not only build the metro rail but would also get a chance to run it for a specified number of years. At the end of this period, the project would either go into government hands or be leased to the contractor for a few more years.) The idea behind pre-qualifying contractors was to root out non-serious contenders from the very beginning.

It was at this stage, in April 2008, that Raju got interested in the metro rail project. This was the time when Harishchandra Prasad came to sell the idea to him. Although Maytas was inducted as a partner along with the Navbharat Group belonging to Prasad's cousin, it soon transpired that Raju's entry was not enough. One of the conditions of the government was that a metro rail operator from anywhere in the world should be part of the consortia. That's how Ital Thai, which had built the elevated twenty-three-kilometre-long Bangkok metro, became part of the

Navbharat–Maytas consortium. Ital Thai was basically a civil and infrastructure company and had no interest in being an operator. But the government in Thailand had no money to pay the company after the metro was built. So instead of paying Ital Thai, it had made it an equity owner in the Bangkok metro project.

In the end, five international consortia that showed an interest in the project were pre-qualified. All of them had foreign partners but were led by Indian groups. There was Anil Ambani's Reliance Energy, which had tied up with Bombardier of Canada; the Essar group in partnership with Singapore Metro Rail; the GVK group with Alstom of France; Nagarjuna Constructions with Siemens of Germany and Magna Allmore; and, of course, the Navbharat–Maytas consortia. The interesting point to note was that Navbharat, and not Raju's Maytas, was the lead partner.

After the consortia were shortlisted and in the run-up to the actual bids, things started changing. One fine day, Harishchandra Prasad found that he had been eased out of the project. Incensed, he went to his cousin, who said: 'What can I do? Raju forced me to push you out.' Prasad called Raju and sought an appointment. Raju was cool. 'Come home in the evening,' he told Prasad. When Prasad met Raju, the latter was his usual unruffled self. 'Oh, are you out of the project? I don't know anything about this. Talk to Ramu,' Raju said, throwing the ball in the court of his brother.

Prasad got the message and did not pursue the matter any more. But Raju had shown his colours once again. Use a man, and when his utility is over, throw him out. Raju was going to mete out the same treatment to the Navbharat Group after the rail project was awarded to the Navbharat–Maytas consortia.

Meanwhile, the Delhi Metro Rail Corporation (DMRC), which had built the highly successful metro rail in the capital city, was roped in as consultant to advise on how to go about the project. Even before the DMRC could complete its studies, the state government began its exercise of marking structures that would have to be demolished to make way for the metro rail project and land that had to be acquired for the purpose.

It was found that roughly over 5,000 commercial units and 2,000 residential units would have to go. Twelve hundred heritage structures would face damage, and old areas like the 300-year-old Sultan Bazar would be completely wiped out. The metro rail would pass very close to the legislative assembly, the Salar Jung museum and other heritage buildings, spoiling the beauty of the area. Not only that, having an elevated metro close to the legislative assembly also had a security angle. A busy commercial centre like Ameerpet, which is always crowded with interstate bus services starting from there, would also give way to the metro rail. It would be here that a huge station complex would be located and the two metro lines would intersect.

The metro rail, it also became apparent, would be at a high level: one of the lines would be at a height of seventy feet or at the level of the seventh floor of an average building, and another at forty-five feet or almost at the level of the fifth floor. There would be platforms at this elevated level to allow people to embark and disembark from the train at stations, which would be at an interval of one kilometre. On top of the platform would be shops and stores because the operator of metro rail was to be allowed to commercially exploit the real estate. In some places – like in the old city of Hyderabad, between Kachiguda and Shahalibanda – even after demolishing buildings, the metro rail would pass within ten to twenty feet of many structures, including homes.

Additionally, there was the sound pollution factor. The metro would run close to schools, colleges, law courts and hospitals, and the sound decibel was likely to exceed permissible levels.

But the government was simply not interested in a debate on this subject. In league with the real estate lobby, the government was in fact trying to hide all details and documents pertaining to the project. It was as if publicizing facts would draw adverse reactions that would force the government to apply a brake on the project.

The only argument being put forward by the metro rail lobby was that commuting time would be reduced in the rapidly expanding city and that distances that normally took two hours to cover could now be covered in just over half an hour. This was, of course, true and the metro rail would be the delight of the middle class, especially those who lived away from the centre of the city. But it would also be a bonanza for people like Raju, whose property/land would greatly appreciate in value because of the project.

Meanwhile, there was frenetic lobbying by influential people to ensure that the metro rail did not cut through their properties or passed close to them. Very soon, this high-voltage lobbying reached even the chief minister's office. Ramalinga Raju was also doing his own calculations, trying to figure out what the project meant for his sizeable landholdings in the city. As usual he kept a low profile; nobody but a close group of his associates knew what he was up to. Most of Raju's land was on the outskirts of the city. In the central section of the metro route, there was no free land: these were older parts of the city which had been developed long time ago. But the lines terminated around the region where Raju's many unlisted companies owned land. And if the lines could be extended later, all the better for Raju. Moreover, real estate development would be possible at the station complex.

After the DMRC came out with a detailed project report, it was realized that the total cost of the metro rail would in fact be higher, at Rs 12,212 crore. Since highly capital intensive projects like metro rail could not start yielding substantial revenues from day one, the Government of India decided to provide a sum of Rs 1,182 crore as viability gap funding (VGF). This was the norm for all urban metros being conceived. The central ministry for urban affairs was headed by Jaipal Reddy. An old Hyderabadi, he agreed to dole out an additional Rs 1,181 crore as central government grant under the Jawaharlal Nehru National Urban Renewal Mission (JNNURM). Seeing this, the Andhra Pradesh government also agreed to shell out the same amount as an outright grant. This left a total of Rs 8,668 crore – not a mean sum – that had to be invested by the project developer.

Even though the project would be awarded on a BOT basis for twenty-five years, could enough revenues be generated to make this highly capital intensive project profitable? Where would the revenues come from? The fare-box collection would obviously not be enough – the fares had been pegged between Rs 8 and Rs 19. The average fare would be Rs 12, double that charged by the MMTS. Some revenues would have to be generated by real estate development to make the project viable. But would that be enough to make the project break even? These were the issues that the pre-qualified contractors were debating amongst themselves.

By the time the bids for the project were called, one of the pre-qualified contractors decided to opt out. The GVK group represented a well-known business group in Hyderabad, and its promoter, G.V. Krishna Reddy, owned a lot of land in and around the city. Three of his properties had been leased out to the Tatas, from where Taj Hotels operated. The group had also won the coveted project to modernize and run the Mumbai airport. But the group, along with its partners Alstom of France and Gammon, decided that there was no way they could make the project work.

The intrepid Raju was, however, having other thoughts. He was trying to figure out if he could beat much bigger players like Reliance and Essar and win the project. That was not going to be easy, but with Raju having made his way into the good books of the ruling party in Andhra Pradesh, Maytas was the hot favourite. There was no way that Raju was going to let this opportunity go by – it would be his biggest catch ever. How could he do it? Raju spent an endless amount of time trying to figure that out. But he had no answer. Meanwhile, someone started a son-of-the-soil argument. 'A big prestigious proposal like this should be awarded to a local party. Why should it be granted to an outsider?' Raju also heard the argument, but realized that no government could award a proposal to a local company just because it was local.

By fair means or foul, his bid had to be the lowest. He had to offer such conditions that no one else could and would. But what could these be? He was competing against bigger companies that had experience in running much bigger projects. Raju realized that he would have to leverage his strength, which came from controlling so much real estate in the city. The Ambanis and Essar could be beaten hollow, because they did not own an acre of land in Hyderabad. But what about GVK and Nagarjuna Construction? Raju had no idea at that time that the GVK group would opt out and he was wary of them.

Raju was also not sure about the Nagarjuna Construction group. This was a company that was owned by another Raju: A.V.S. Raju. What is more, A.V.S. and Ramalinga had done extensive business together, which included the modernization of Gulbarga and Shimoga airports. In fact, the two had at least three joint venture companies amongst themselves. How much would A.V.S. Raju bid? Raju hadn't the foggiest idea. But it was essential for him to know all this, for how else could he bid successfully for the project?

Then Raju had a brainwave – it was actually suggested by somebody high up in the government: if only he could structure the project in such a way that instead of seeking VGF from the centre, he could instead promise to pay a yearly licence fee, he was bound to win the deal. For one, nobody would be reckless enough to pay money to the government where the latter was actually willing to shell out funds! Secondly, by promising to not take central government subsidy, he could shrug New Delhi off his back. So long as the centre was not coughing up funds, it wouldn't be bothered about how the developer was executing the projects. As far as the state government was concerned, Raju knew how to handle it.

Raju saw this as a chance to project himself as a hero – the one who gave Hyderabad its metro rail for free, without any tax money and all at his own expense. Of course, there would be a huge cost in terms of dislocation of residences and businesses. Land acquisition would not be without considerable costs both in terms of money and time, but then Raju had not given a thought to all these things.

The bids for the Hyderabad metro rail were called on 23 July 2008, and when the offer documents were opened, it was found that the Maytas consortium had offered to pay a huge Rs 1,350 crore to the government as licence money for being awarded the project. In sharp contrast, Anil Ambani's Reliance Energy had sought Rs 2,811 crore from the government for building the rail, and the Essar group wanted Rs 3,100 crore for the same. G.V.K. Raju did not bid, and Nagarjuna Construction, headed by A.V.S. Raju, offered Rs 152 crore to the government. A.V.S. Raju had the same idea as Ramalinga Raju but then he did not have the recklessness and enterprise of the latter to pull it off.

On 28 July, the decision of the tender evaluation committee was announced: the Maytas consortium would develop and run the project for thirty-five years. After this, it was possible to extend the term of the project by another twenty-five years. The consortium would leverage eighteen to twenty lakh square feet of real estate available around metro rail stations for commercial development and this would ensure a sizeable revenue stream. A total of 269 acres of land would be available to the project developer, and this included huge chunks of land in prime areas like Punjagutta and upcoming prime areas like Miyapur.

On 1 August 2008, the Andhra Pradesh cabinet gave its approval to the project, even as there was consternation among the public and the bidders, who were clueless about how the Maytas consortium could actually promise such a huge sum to the state government. But even before the cabinet could approve the project, the consortium floated a company named Maytas Metro Private Limited to implement it.

On 17 September, two days before the 'concession agreement' was signed, the company was made into a public limited company called Maytas Metro. Significantly, even though the three companies, Maytas, Navbharat and Ital Thai, had jointly bid for the project, the names of the other two companies were not reflected anywhere in the newly floated enterprise. Also, these two companies were not given substantial shares in Maytas Metro Limited, reflecting the fact that Ramalinga Raju was the man who had swung the deal in favour of the consortium. Thus, the Rajus were going to be the real bosses of the project. The promoter of Maytas Metro was none other than Raju's very own Maytas Infra, which held 44,995 of the 50,000 shares of the company. The other shareholders included his elder son, Teja, and wife, Nandini.

The government order granting the project to the Maytas consortium was issued on 8 August, and simultaneously, Line 1, which ran from Shilparaman in Hi Tech City to Habsiguda near

Osmania University, was extended by a few more kilometres to Nagole. The ostensible reason was that Osmania University was refusing to part with land required to set up a rail depot. So perforce, the authorities had to extend the line to Nagole, where there was government land available on which the depot would come up. There were, however, not many takers for this argument – it was believed that the extension was made to favour a big realtor who had a real estate project in the neighbourhood of Nagole. For a change, the realtor was not Ramalinga Raju, but the point is that many land sharks were looking for a kill from the metro rail project.

The Andhra Pradesh government spent the whole month of August in creating conditions that would help Raju and his companies with the metro rail project. In line with this, in an unprecedented development, the state government passed a new Tramways Act. Among other things, as per this act, the tramway operator (the metro rail was classified as a tramway operation to bypass the regulations of the Indian Railways, which otherwise would seek a role in determining the terms offered to the operator) was empowered to acquire public or private land and immovable properties if it was in the interest of the implementation of the metro rail.

This was not all that the Rajasekhara Reddy regime did for Ramalinga Raju. It went ahead and took upon itself an obligation to procure sites (all land and buildings) required by Raju within thirty to sixty days of Maytas depositing its performance security of Rs 260 crore for the project. The performance security was to be deposited within six months of the deal being signed. The Andhra Pradesh government also promised to obtain within this stipulated period all permissions from the railway authorities for building bridges over existing railway lines.

What is more interesting, the state government took it upon itself to pay a penalty of Rs 24 lakh (subject to a maximum of Rs 48 crore) for each day's delay in procuring land or rail approval. This was a nearly impossible task for the government. For instance, it was just not possible to get railway approvals within two months, not the least because the metro rail line would pass over all the ten platforms of the Secunderabad railway station. The railways would hardly entertain such a proposal: it had earlier scoffed at other minor proposals made by the state government and had taken an inordinately long time to clear them. It was also impossible to brave public outcry and acquire all the land required in densely populated areas of Hyderabad in just over seven to eight months. Thus it was clear that the Andhra Pradesh government was entering into an agreement knowing fully well that cash from the exchequer would have to be transferred to Maytas. This would be over and above the grant of Rs 1,181 crore.

Added to this, the government of Andhra Pradesh was also ready to forgo future revenues to Maytas. It undertook not to subject metro rail-related real estate development to any form of municipal taxes and other local duties. Thereby, more profits were being ensured for Ramalinga at the cost of funds to the city municipality. In other words, with the metro rail deal, Raju was being given unfettered powers over real estate in Hyderabad. It was a dream come true for him. He was becoming the uncrowned king of the city, the virtual Nizam of Hyderabad.

Though there was a sense of disquiet amongst losing bidders, things were okay for a month. The prime reason was that the government was acting in great secrecy and not many knew the full details of the deal being entered into. Raju's social status was going up. Many were praising him and there were even suggestions that the line that ran to Hi Tech City be extended by another ten kilometres to Gachibowli, which was fast emerging as a technology hub with companies like Microsoft, Infosys and the Indian School of Business having their campuses there. Gachibowli was becoming a hot spot, but not long ago it was all wilderness. Raju's unlisted companies had picked up land in these areas, and were even trying to acquire disputed land. (In one instance, Teja Raju personally went and met the vice chancellor of the University of Hyderabad, located in Gachibowli, to convince him to part with land belonging to the university that was caught in a legal tangle.) An extension of the metro rail to that area would skyrocket the price of the real estate that he controlled.

In Delhi, the deputy chairman of the Planning Commission, Montek Singh Ahluwalia, was upholding Hyderabad Metro as a shining example of how an urban transit system could be created without dipping into the kitty of the central government. 'We are not going to give funds any more to any metros coming up anywhere in the country. If Hyderabad can do it, other cities can jolly well do it too,' Ahluwalia declared at various interactions. Things were looking good for Raju, but it was too good to last.

The Delhi Metro Rail chairman, E. Sreedharan, was not amused at the turn of events. Considered the father of metro rail in India, to the technocrat it was obvious that there was more than met the eye in the awarding of the metro rail project. The honest metro man decided to write to Montek Singh Ahluwalia and point out the incongruity in the whole affair. Sreedharan wrote: 'Making available 269 acres of prime land free of cost to the BOT operator for commercial exploitation is like selling the family silver… A big political scandal will ensue out of this… It is apparent that the BOT operator has a hidden agenda which appears to be to extend the metro network to a large tract of his private landholdings so as to reap a windfall profit of four to five times the land price.' Sreedharan continued: 'Free land can be given to partly fund the project, but it should not be more than 7 to 8 per cent of the project cost.'

The metro man concluded by saying that this was a 'real estate project, not a metro project'. Sreedharan also clarified that although DMRC had been consultants to the project, it was not involved in the evaluation of bids or extension of routes. He also said that to make a project like Hyderabad's metro rail viable, the central government would have to dole out 40 per cent of the costs as VGF.

Pandemonium broke out the moment bits of Sreedharan's report found their way into the press. Smartly, Raju did not make a single comment in public about the volley of firepower that was directed against him. He did not need to bother: the Andhra Pradesh government was taking up cudgels on his behalf. The finance minister of Andhra Pradesh, K. Rosaiah, called a press conference threatening to sue Sreedharan for his report and asked him to tender an apology. Sreedharan, of course, did nothing of that sort. The government of Andhra Pradesh, which was merely posturing, could not pick up the courage to challenge the metro man in court.

The government's perspective was given to me by the managing director of the metro project, N.V.S. Reddy. 'In such projects there is always strong opposition from some quarter or the other. There are vested interests and there are people who are unable to appreciate the big picture. There are lobbies and counter lobbies who raise objections, some of which may not be relevant. Our government was guided by the best interests of the people of Hyderabad and the most that we can be accused of is being proactive in trying to provide the city with a first-rate urban transit system.'

As mentioned earlier, Maytas had been granted the project on the basis of the experience that Ital Thai had in implementing a metro project (in Bangkok). However, once the deal was signed, Ital Thai seemed to be out of the project (a PIL in this regard was filed in the Andhra Pradesh high court. But before the PIL could be heard, the metro deal with Maytas was scrapped). This was tantamount to making a mockery of the tender conditions and favouring Raju through the backdoor. But no one in the corridors of power was interested in taking cognizance of this.

After Raju went to jail, his elder son, Teja, tried to push forward the rail project. But Maytas was unable to cough up the performance guarantee of Rs 260 crore that it had to pay to the state government and sought an extension – first of three months and then of six months – to pay up. The state government, caught in its own trap of awarding the project to a consortium clearly incapable of implementing the project, did not know what to do. With the ensuing general and state elections, the matter went on the backburner. Meanwhile, Teja Raju moved heaven and earth to rope in new companies to partner him in the deal and bring in finance. However, all of them backed off, realizing that the project was just not financially viable because of the large sums promised by Maytas to the government.

On 7 July 2009, even as Maytas sought another six months' extension to pay up after almost a year of having won the contract, the powers that be ran out of patience. The Andhra Pradesh state government finally issued an order scrapping the contract. Fresh bids are now being called. Teja Raju says that in the aftermath of the Satyam crisis, Maytas's business and size has shrunk. 'If we were big enough, I would have bid again,' he says. As it turned out, the Rajus have been divested of their control of Maytas Infra. Among the companies which are applying for the rail project are Anil Ambani's Reliance, the GVK Group and Essar.

SEVEN

The Great Siphoning Off

Promoters like Ramalinga Raju, who live on the edge, are a breed apart. For them the companies they control are milch cows – *kamadhenus* that must be milked. So long as a company yields cash, it's fine. Once that stops, they go on to build another company that can be similarly milked.

Thus, instead of nurturing Satyam, Ramalinga Raju is suspected to have leveraged the shares he owned to pump his company dry.

Raju did so by taking advantage of the ascending stock market, which led to a rapid increase in the share prices of Satyam. The suspicion is that the money was diverted to other purposes that were possibly not wholly legitimate, such as his land deals or investments overseas. Raju often sold the shares at great risk because, as we have seen, over the years his control over Satyam (in terms of equity holding) got greatly reduced. (By the end of 2008, barely a week before he gave in, his shareholding had come down to 2 per cent.)

The lure of the lucre was so overpowering for Raju that he forgot to take his cue from the promoters of Infosys and Wipro, two companies with whom he continually compared Satyam. Azim Premji would have been a more apt example to follow as his business was like Raju's – a family-owned enterprise – unlike Infosys, whose promoters were a group of professionals led by N.R. Narayana Murthy. Azim Premji, on paper, owns over 70 per cent of the equity of the company and is reputed to control over 80 per cent of Wipro indirectly.

Raju also did not go the way of other Indian IT czars such as Shiv Nadar of HCL Technologies and Rajendra Pawar of NIIT. They too hold a much higher percentage of the equity in their own companies (Nadar, along with associates, held nearly 75 per cent of HCL in 2004). The promoters of Tech Mahindra – the company that has now taken over Satyam – own over 83 per cent. But Raju did the very reverse of what Premji and others did: he went on disinvesting from his own company.

In the good old days, when business was run on trust, Indian promoters managed their enterprises while themselves holding barely 10 per cent of the company's equity. The major part of the equity was normally held by public financial institutions that took the role of sleeping partners and allowed the promoters to run the company in the manner they wished to. There were, of course, a large number of shareholders, each holding a minuscule part of the equity of the company. They were never in a position to influence the course that the company took. In these circumstances, the promoter was the king.

The alarm bells started ringing in the early 1980s, when NRI industrialist Swraj Paul made an almost successful bid to take over two prominent companies: the DCM and Escorts. For the first time, public financial institutions – under instructions from political powers – showed their preference for a corporate raider, sending shivers down the spine of promoters all across corporate India. Swraj Paul put the entire spectrum of promoters on notice by announcing that they could not run their companies as private empires on public money.

Though Paul's takeover attempt was stymied, promoters realized that the time had come to consolidate their holdings. In the new scenario, promoters figured that they should have control over at least 30 per cent of the shareholding of the company to stave off any takeover attempt. Slowly but surely, they started working towards this objective and their resolve strengthened in the wake of the new Security and Exchange Board (SEBI) regulations regarding takeovers in 1994. Three years later, a new takeover code was unveiled, and following this many companies that had earlier thought it prudent to hold about 30 per cent shares in the enterprise they promoted, scrambled to raise their stakes to at least 40 per cent. Many of them went further, resting only after their stake had gone up to 50.51 per cent.

The only exceptions were companies with a huge equity base and lakhs of shareholders, each holding a minuscule part of the total equity. But even here, the companies preferred to be conservative: Mukesh Ambani and his associates own over 49 per cent of the equity of Reliance Industries and the holdings of Ratan Tata and others top 40 per cent of the equity of Tata Steel.

Ramalinga Raju went for his maiden public issue of Satyam in 1992, barely a year after the Narasimha Rao government had embarked on the path of liberalization. Satyam was just a fledgling company at that time and had nothing that would attract any corporate takeover attempt. Further, technology was yet to become the flavour of the times. For new entrepreneurs such as Raju, the attempt was to sell more shares of the company to the public because that would lead to infusion of funds into the enterprise for its various expansion plans.

Thus, the initial public offering resulted in limiting the shares of the promoter group led by Ramalinga Raju to merely 18.78 per cent or 34,89,000 shares, leaving 81.22 per cent of the equity in the market. Other than Ramalinga Raju, the promoter group included his wife, Nandini, brothers Rama and Suryanarayana, his father, Satyanarayana, his mother, Appalanarasamma, and the wives of his brothers, Radha and Jhansi Rani. Satyam Construction, which was started in 1988, was also a promoter of Satyam Computer Services. So was its first managing director, D.V.S. Raju, who was soon eased out of the company.

By 1995, liberalization policies had started yielding results and had raised the Indian economy to a high growth track. Even though the pace of new reforms had started slowing, it was clear that the process was there to stay. This meant that the stock markets would continue to boom and that money could be made from speculation on the bourses. What was more, Raju realized that he could indirectly speculate on his own shares. The IPO had enabled him to establish contacts with many brokers on the stock exchanges, and in any case, running a public limited company with listed shares brings promoters in constant touch with folks who deal in the market.

To realize his goal of making money through trading in his own shares, Raju set up five investment companies in May 1995: Elem Investments, High Grace Investments, High Sound Investments (the name of this company was later changed to SNR Investments), Finicity Investments and Veeyes Investments. Though there is nothing illegal in company promoters and directors trading in their own shares, they must not violate the norms of insider trading established by SEBI. These norms prevent company directors from using 'price sensitive' information to speculate in shares.

By 1997, trading was in full swing and now Ramalinga Raju's two sons, Teja Raju and Rama Raju Jr, had also been inducted into the promoter's group. But if Raju was selling shares of Satyam through these investment companies, he was also buying some of them, including those of Satyam, from the market. As a result, the promoters' shareholding was actually creeping up, going up to 19.76 per cent in October 1997. But after that, Raju's shareholding started falling. Two years later, in 1999, the promoters were allotted bonus shares (a process in which additional shares are allotted to shareholders for a price that is usually below the market price) amounting to a total of 44,18,602 shares. By now, the total number of shares held by the Rajus was 89,30,606, or 17.34 per cent of the total shares of the company.

In a way, 1999 was the watershed year in the Raju story. This was the year he graduated to the big league of financial games. The stock market was rising and the tech boom had set in. Raju realized that this was the time to go for the kill. He started with the weakest link in his promoters group – his mother, Appalanarasamma, who stayed at home and had no clue about what her son was doing. He sold off the shares of Satyam that were in her name. The next in line were Raju's younger brother, Suryanarayana Raju, who had not gone beyond intermediate college, and his wife, Jhansi Rani.

In order to ensure that market analysts did not get a whiff of the fact that promoters were selling off their shares (for that would have led to a fall in prices of Satyam's shares), Raju got hold of seventeen loyal employees in his company who belonged to his own community. After convincing them – and this was not difficult considering that they thought of Ramalinga as a god – the shares of Appalanarasamma, Suryanarayana and Jhansi Rani were endorsed (technically with their knowledge) in the names of these employees and their family members.

In turn, the employees lodged these endorsed shares into their demat accounts (this allows paper transactions of shares without actual physical delivery and is the preferred mode of trading these days) and offloaded them in the market through the five investment companies that Raju had set up. Naturally, after selling the shares, the investment companies transferred the proceeds to the demat accounts, and through backward movement these amounts came back to Raju's mother, brother and his brother's wife.

Raju was heady after the sale. He had made money, and nobody had even suspected that he had. Even his mother, brother, and his brother's wife did not realize (if they ever found this out or protested is not known) that they now held lesser number of shares of Satyam. Raju was at the helm at Satyam, but on paper, he had other family members as partners. Now, with lesser shares, their hold over Satyam would gradually loosen.

Next year, in 2000, Raju decided to repeat the exercise. This time, the remaining shares of his mother, brother and his brother's wife were sold off. The shares of his father too were offloaded in the market. The exercise took place in the same way in which it had taken place earlier. When asked by the father about the logic behind the offloading, Raju told him that in his estimation, the tech boom wouldn't last too long, so it made sense to exit the company as fast as possible.

Anyway, as a family they were more interested in real estate, so it made sense to skim the cream from technology and put it into land. To avoid suspicion, Raju also got his younger son to sell off his shares of Satyam, along with those of his youngest brother's wife, Radha, and son, Pritham. But all this was a subterfuge devised by Raju in which his youngest brother was with him. This is clear from the fact that after the sales, the proceeds that accrued to his mother, father, brother Suryanarayana and his wife were all 'gifted' to Ramalinga Raju, Rama Raju, and their respective wives. The gift – a hefty one – amounted to almost Rs 75.69 crore! What the quid pro quo was is not known. Appalanarasamma knew nothing about the affairs of business and neither did Jhansi. But even with his little education, Suryanarayana would have understood, and Raju may have worked out an arrangement with him.

But Raju was not just making money by selling shares. He was allegedly siphoning off money from Satyam by sophisticated and elaborate swindling techniques. In one instance – detected by the income tax department – he transferred approximately Rs 19.5 crore to the bank accounts of his mother, father and other elderly relatives of his extended family. Income tax laws in India exempt banks from subjecting deposits of senior citizens to TDS.

So not only was Raju swindling funds, he was also parking them in the names of senior citizens so that he would not have to pay taxes on them. When the matter was discovered, the Rajus used every trick in the book to put the investigating income tax official (an honest young lady called S. Padmaja) off the track. This included various intimidation tactics, and once, when the official went to the Satyam office to check documents, she was locked in a room for a few hours. Ultimately, Raju used high-level political pressure to hush up the case and escaped by paying income tax on this amount, which should have rightly been confiscated. Those in the know of things allege that the Rajus siphoned off funds in other ways too, but no government official had the courage to unravel such matters. Padmaja, who nailed the Rajus, was transferred for doing so. But her bosses, who pressured her to stop the investigations, flourished and are now in important positions in the tax department. A retired boss was even rewarded with a high public office.

After making Rs 75 crore by selling Satyam shares belonging to his extended family, Raju's appetite was whetted. By now the Raju family shareholding in Satyam had gone down to 12.88 per cent. He thought it was worth it to dispose of the family's entire shareholding of Satyam gradually. Nobody would notice because the offloading would be in tranches and this sale would be relegated to an inconspicuous corner of the company's balance sheet.

Moreover, if the shareholding of the promoter's group was going down, Raju could always make Satyam issue bonus shares – in the name of raising funds for the company. Thus, in effect, Raju's control on Satyam would remain as it was. In any case, the shareholding of Satyam was sufficiently dispersed and nobody really owned a big chunk of the company's shares.

So began the process of accelerated divestment of Satyam shares. By 2006, the shareholding of the Raju group had fallen to 8.59 per cent of the total equity. In return, Ramalinga Raju made a real killing. The promoter family had made a staggering Rs 707 crore by selling 1.09 crore shares as per the investigations of the CBI, though there was nothing illegal about this.

For all these years, these facts remained hidden in the maze of paperwork. This is not surprising given how opaque corporate governance in India is. But the sleuths of Serious Frauds Investigations Office (SFIO), a new organization that works under the aegis of the Government of India's department of company affairs, figured out that the Raju family had made a much higher amount out of these transactions. The Rajus made a total of Rs 3,029 crore by selling 3.91 crore shares, according to SFIO. And Raju himself raked in Rs 773 crore.

Irrespective of how much Raju and his family members made, the goose which laid the golden eggs was still very much alive. In 2006, Raju allotted bonus shares and 2,78,67,000 shares came the way of the promoter family. The total number of shares owned by the promoters was 5,57,36,000. Obviously there was still much more scope to make money.

A new phase of fleecing Satyam began in 2006, with Raju setting up a new holding company called SRSR Holdings. All the shares of Ramalinga Raju and Rama Raju, along with those of their respective wives, were transferred to this company. The transfer took place through four major block deals on 14 September that year at a price ranging between Rs 809 to 817 per share, each of face value of Rs 2. The transfer of the shares to SRSR Holdings would make any further sale easy. Nobody would realize that the Rajus were selling off Satyam shares. It would appear that SRSR Holdings was disposing of the shares. And nobody really knew anything about this company.

The irony of the situation is that the less fortunate brother, Suryanarayana Raju, whose shares in Satyam had already been disposed of by Raju and whose proceeds he had appropriated, was asked to run this company. Raju was cold-blooded and dominated his brother. The latter obeyed every order of his brother even though he had perhaps not been given his due. To ensure that things did not go out of control, Raju also appointed his own sons as directors of SRSR Holdings. Simultaneously, another company, SRSR Advisory Services (Pvt) Ltd, was also established. This company was to give legal, secretarial and other help in the sell-off operations, and assist the 327 privately held companies that Raju had spawned since 1999. Again, Suryanarayana Raju was made the titular in-charge of SRSR Advisory. In fact, he was given the power of attorney to deal with all matters of the company.

Ramalinga Raju had become smarter. He was not going to just sell his shares. His plan now was to have his cake and eat it too. The new game was to raise money by pledging the shares to nonbanking finance corporations (NBFCs). He would have to keep the shares as collateral with these companies and, in return, he would get funds. Of course, he had to pay interest for borrowing this money, but that was okay with Raju. With the stock market appreciating rapidly, the whole affair turned out to be a double bonanza for him. This was because with increasing scrip prices, the shares he pledged became worth much more. And when that happened, Raju could raise more funds against them.

In the event, as much as Rs 1,744 crore was raised between 2006 and 2008 by keeping the shares of Satyam that were owned by SRSR Holdings as collateral. The shares were pledged with a host of NBFCs such as Deutsche Investments (Pvt) Ltd, DSP Merrill Lynch, GE Capital Services and the State Investment Corporation of Maharashtra (SICOM). But the most interesting thing is that the money that was obtained by keeping the shares pledged was not coming directly to Ramalinga Raju. Instead, it was going to the host of private companies that he had set up since 1999 to buy land in and around Hyderabad. The companies which benefitted were Harangi Agro, Amravati Agro, Vyaya Agro, Samudra Bangar Agro Farms, Vamadeva Agro and Pavithravati Agro.

For the record, however, after he was arrested, Raju told his interrogators that the money raised by these companies was ploughed back into Satyam. This was necessary, Raju told the police, because Satyam did not have the revenues and profits that it was projected to have. This is also what he had said in his confession letter. But this is more likely to be an attempt to pull the wool over the eyes of investigators – a move to confess to a lesser crime and escape punishment for a graver offence. Falsifying books is certainly a lesser crime than siphoning off funds from a company.

However, analysts agree that fudging had taken place in Satyam, and even though it was substantial, Raju did not find it necessary to infuse funds into the company. The fudging had the result of portraying Satyam in a better light. As a result, Satyam's shares were quoted in the market at a price higher than what was justified. Since Raju sold off the shares, he was the beneficiary of the higher prices.

Raju seems to have managed to convince the CBI that his crime was basically to inflate his books of account – and not siphon off funds – and in their interim charge sheet, the investigation agency has more or less proceeded on the same lines as Raju in his confession letter. But investigations are still on, and it is possible that the CBI will stumble upon other facts.

Already, the Enforcement Directorate has found that funds from Satyam were used by the Rajus to buy 287 properties in Hyderabad, Bangalore, Chennai and Nagpur between the years 2005 and 2009. The properties were purchased in the name of eighty privately owned companies belonging to the Rajus. A sum of Rs 170 crore was used to buy these properties although their present market value would be much higher. What is interesting is that most of the properties were shown as agricultural land in the records, although most of them were in urban areas. It is expected that more will be heard on these matters in the months to come.

It may also be noted that no record has been found in the Satyam files that testifies to a sum of Rs 1,425 crore being infused by the Rajus' privately held companies in Satyam, as claimed by them after Ramalinga's confession. In fact, to make their argument stronger, Suryanarayana Raju wrote to the Satyam management on 8 January 2009 – a day after Raju confessed and resigned from the company – demanding that the money be paid back. This letter seems to have been written at Raju's instance, an attempt to weave a story post facto that would entail a lesser punishment for him.

As a shareholder of Satyam, Raju also legitimately made money out of Satyam: this is through dividends that were declared from time to time. As per data available, Raju and other members of his promoter group made over Rs 115 crore as dividend from the year 1994 (when dividend was declared for the first time) till the time Raju exited the company. Of this, Raju personally made Rs 21 crore and Rama Raju Rs 24 crore. These amounts don't seem to be much, but then this was legitimate income. Suryanarayana also made Rs 1.80 crore and his wife nearly Rs 42 lakh. Raju's wife made almost Rs 9 crore.

Many Indian businessmen do not remit their entire export incomes back to the country. But instances of Indian corporates not bringing back the funds they raise from foreign bourses must be very few. Satyam was perhaps one of them. At least that is what the investigations of the SFIO are now revealing. In 2001, Raju went to the NYSE and listed Satyam's scrip on the bourse, taking advantage of the tech boom and the name that Indian software companies were making for themselves. But the money raised (Rs 760 crore) from the American Depository Share (ADS) was not remitted to India. Raju's men deposited the money in Citibank's New York branch, from where it was transferred to Citibank's Bahrain branch. But from here only Rs 397 crore was brought back to India by Satyam. The rest of the money was transferred to some unknown accounts, which the Indian law enforcing agencies have not been able to trace till now.

The CBI has also zeroed in on three accounts in the US owned by American citizens. Cash worth Rs 80 crore was diverted to these accounts by Satyam. The background of these Americans is, however, yet to be established, and the CBI has requested the help of the Interpol to proceed further on this matter.

SFIO's investigation also seems to suggest that the inward remittance of Satyam's export incomes was also suspect. Possibly, a part of Satyam's export incomes was diverted to tax havens like Mauritius and brought back to India. But this money – which legitimately belonged to Satyam's shareholders – did not come back to the company. It possibly found its way to Raju's interests outside Satyam, most likely to land purchases.

The suspicion is that the funds were diverted to buy real estate in Andhra Pradesh, Tamil Nadu, Maharashtra and Karnataka. In Hyderabad, fifty plots of land were purchased in Medchal and Qutbullapur. It is believed that Satyam's account in Bank of Baroda's New York branch was used to divert the money. Fictitious fixed deposits were created to show that Satyam had a large amount of cash. But in reality, it was spirited away. All this, however, is yet to be proven.

EIGHT

A Bundle of Contradictions

Those who have known Ramalinga Raju for long or have worked with him at close quarters swear that he has a duality of character – he can be the friendly, benevolent Dr Jekyll as well as the evil Mr Hyde. But there is a caveat. Most people never saw his corrupt side, though there might have been an indication or two. On display almost always was Dr Jekyll, immersed perpetually in work, yet concerned about his employees and the society he lived in.

Raju's image was that of an introvert, a poor conversationalist and a boring and indifferent public speaker. 'It was not easy to strike a conversation with him at a party or elsewhere. He would say nothing on his own and would answer only in monosyllables. So how do you figure him out?' asks a businessman who has known him for long. 'He was the epitome of good behaviour, spoke softly and criticized nobody. We used to wonder how a person so high in life could be so humble,' says another businessman who met him a couple of times.

'He had specialist knowledge over a narrow range of subjects and if you tapped that, he would talk incessantly,' says a retired chairman of a multinational. This narrow groove in which his domain expertise lay included management subjects like leadership, philosophy of business and planning for the future. 'Though he did not talk much, you did not come off after meeting him with a bad feeling. He exuded positive vibes,' says a senior corporate manager.

Besides being a private person, Raju was also very hardworking. His senior colleagues say that he could well be described as a workaholic. 'Once not too long ago, both of us arrived in Hyderabad in the early hours of the morning after a journey from the US. A meeting had been fixed for 7 a.m. I did not go for the meeting assuming that it would be cancelled. But I was told that Raju reached there, right on time. No jet lag for him,' recollects one of his colleagues. 'He was known to sleep between 11 p.m. and 5 a.m. At any other hour, managers could expect to get calls from him, seeking detailed information on various matters,' a Satyam manager says.

At one level, Raju was a slave driver pushing his managers hard (though his style was to nag people rather than order them about) for results. But at another level, he was a highly liberal boss. Satyam always had surplus staff and a large number of people on the bench. Raju thought nothing of the many Satyam employees having fun at the company's expense, running up huge tour bills and going for private work during office hours. He was quite aware that a few employees were swiping in attendance for some of their colleagues. But he did not seem to mind this. 'It may sound surprising but that is how it was. Raju never pulled up any manager for running the business in an unprofessional manner. He never told them that he would sack them for non-performance,' says a senior Satyam executive. In other words, he could be contradictory – nagging his managers on the one hand and turning a blind eye to their laxity at work on the other.

Having spent his early days in a small place where caste, clan and kin mattered a lot, Raju was a family man, except that in his case it was an extended family. He viewed his own company as one big family and even hired teams of husbands and wives. Modern management theories suggest that employing couples might add an altogether unsavoury dimension to office politics, but Raju's theory was that it would be a good way to cut attrition.

The flip side was that Raju hired a lot of men from his own caste. Also, though he never spelt it out explicitly, Raju obviously felt that as a Telugu icon he had to recruit a lot of Telugus. Many of his senior managers were given a free hand in hiring extensively from their home districts in Andhra Pradesh. This helped connect to local communities and established strong ties for the company. Interestingly, while top IT companies were quite strict about the marks scored by fresh recruits in academics, Satyam was happy to make relaxations. After 2001, he started the practice of granting Rs 1 lakh to all 'Byrraju' girls (Ramalinga Raju's full name is Byrraju Ramalinga Raju, Byrraju standing for his surname) at the time of marriage.

What also made Raju a traditionalist was the fact that he did not have the benefit of a good school education. His father was ambitious but not very well educated, and roamed the state trying to build a grape farming business. Of course, the family would be in tow, and education was not the top priority in rural communities. This accounts for the half a dozen schools that Raju went to, most of them in moffusil areas. He studied up to class III in Bhimavaram, a small town in West Godavari district, which then had a population of a few thousand people. The next three years of schooling were done in Machilipatnam, an old port city in Krishna district. For the next three years, till class

IX, Raju studied in Hyderabad. He did his class X in the very remote Yendakandiga, a small subdivisional hamlet in the West Godavari district. Raju was never good at studies, and the fact that he went to nondescript schools did nothing to showcase any promise. Though they were not poor, the Rajus lived in a house that cannot be called modern by any standards. But then those were not the days of conspicuous consumption, and even the rich did not live ostentatiously.

By 1970, Raju's father had become prosperous and aspired to give his sons a good education. So Ramalinga Raju was packed off to the Andhra Loyola College in Vijayawada. This was a fairly new college established by the Jesuit fathers just a decade and a half earlier. Raju finished his intermediate from this college and went on to acquire a B.Com. This was in 1975. But Raju was still a rudderless young man and hadn't a clue about what to do next in life. His father was by now more established. He knew that going up the social hierarchy was an important part of life. One way of doing this was to ape the ways of the smart set. He realized that education in the US was the flavour of the times, and a degree in management was most sought after.

Satyanarayana pushed Raju – over whom he exercised a lot of control – to do an MBA in the US. Raju got admission to the Ohio University in Athens and one can imagine his sense of bewilderment when he landed there. To say that it was a cultural leap for the boy is an understatement. Ramalinga's life and values began to change in this country of opportunities. He soon realized that he was rather naïve and knew nothing about the ways of the modern world. His own inadequacies began to worry him. But a new world had opened up for Raju and he started absorbing whatever he saw there. It also made an introvert out of him: he had little confidence to face this new world. At the end of his MBA course, Raju felt that there was more to learn, and he wanted to do an MA in economics. But his father was not keen and called him back home. For Satyanarayana, going abroad and acquiring a degree was good enough. Learning was not exactly what he was looking for.

So Ramalinga Raju came back home to Hyderabad, where his father had set up home. Soon thereafter his grandfather (also called Rama Raju) died. This caused much agony to Ramalinga as he was very attached to him. A few months later, Raju got married. It was an arranged marriage: the girl was beautiful and came from a well-to-do family. Nandini had done her graduation in economics from Osmania University in Hyderabad. Her father was a mechanical engineer who had worked for some years in Germany. Apparently, a top industrialist of the Raju community wanted his daughter to marry Ramalinga. But that did not happen as Ramalinga had seen Nandini and wanted to marry her. It was 1977 and Raju was merely twenty-three years odd. Raju started helping out his father in his business, and a few years later, founded his own enterprise. He named it Sri Satyam Spinning Mills, after his father, Satyanarayana. He was steeped in a tradition that accorded an almost godlike stature to one's parents. (When Satyanarayana died at the end of June 2001, Ramalinga in a matter of days set up the Byrraju Foundation to work for rural upliftment and perpetuate the memory of his father.) Raju's youngest brother, Rama Raju, joined him in his business after a couple of years. Though not as introverted as Raju, Ramu treated him with the utmost respect and tried to emulate him.

If spending two years in the US had opened up Raju's mind, the success of Satyam marked a second change in his personality. Though Satyam was started with the prompting and participation of his techie cousin, D.V.S. Raju, Ramalinga Raju had got rid of him by 1992. Raju realized that he would have to build contacts in the US on his own and would have to learn the rudiments of technology. What better way to do this than to spend some time at the Harvard Business School? And so the next year, Raju was in the US again for a course in advanced management offered to presidents/owners of companies.

Raju's outlook changed at Harvard – his mental horizon expanded and he got a chance to network with many business leaders who were taking the course or had taken it in the past. It was after he came back from Harvard that Raju started spewing management jargon. He had also become more confident, not the least because his business had started taking off. Over the next few years, Raju's proclivity for looking at everything through the prism of management philosophy increased.

But at the core, the transformation was phoney because he was hiding things all the time. He had to be very careful about what he was saying. 'This was not clear to us then, but when we look back this is apparent. At meetings – especially in large groups – he would never give direct answers. He would listen to the question carefully, but would pause for a long time before answering. He would be very thoughtful. There was nothing spontaneous about him,' a senior HR executive from Satyam says. He adds: 'I did not report directly to Raju, but I understand that even in smaller meetings Raju would often answer slowly.' The most interesting episodes would happen in large group meetings, where Raju would ask for questions in writing. A few days later, he would reply to the questions over email!

After 2000, when Satyam had entered the big league, Raju began to talk more about leadership. It was at this time that he felt that he needed another 'American dose'. The dot com bubble had burst and Raju figured out that he needed to study the scenario at first-hand. This time he packed his bags and decided to migrate lock, stock and barrel to New Jersey (also taking with him his domestic help and cook!). 'Satyam's major markets are in the US. What's the point of our being here? I should be where my customers are,' Raju told his wife. With the communications network having improved, Raju ran Satyam from the US. But a year later, Raju was back home. His father died at this time and 9/11 also happened. Raju felt more comfortable in Hyderabad. 'After he came back to India, he was like a virtual immigrant. He propounded the theory that in this era of globalization, where the world was becoming one, it did not make any difference where you lived. But your mindset should be global,' says a close associate.

Although Raju wanted to be a virtual immigrant with a global mindset, his mind was hardly global. This mind seemed rooted in the ways of his West Godavari district. He was a bundle of contradictions – on the one hand he was trying to adapt his company and himself to global conditions, on the other he continued to be feudal and provincial in his approach. This accounts for his hunger for land such as is seen in feudal societies where land is the source of income and the quantum of land owned the only benchmark of status. Some senior executives of Satyam say that even as an IT czar he often showed a 'desire' to own land that they found strange. 'I was part of the team responsible for the establishment of our Nagpur development centre. We came back and reported to Raju that we had got the government's permission and had secured 100 acres of land. Raju's reaction was, "Why only 100 acres. Could we not get more land?" He asked us to go back and prospect around for more land,' a top manager of Satyam says. It was this quest for land that took Raju to Gujarat, where he was able to wangle twenty-eight acres of prime land from Narendra Modi in Gandhinagar.

Back from the US in 2001, Raju realized that there was a severe leadership crisis in the company in the upper and middle management rungs. He wanted to implement at Satyam all the practices he had seen in the US. He kicked off a leadership school in the company and told his staff: 'Satyam is a global brand and you should see it as such. We are not a local company. We must transcend local cultures and become a multicultural company.' Other management lessons also came to Satyam employees, courtesy Raju. 'The cost advantage got our foot in the door. Then we added quality. Now we need innovation. Fifteen years ago it was about how many lines of codes and at what cost. Now it's no longer about technology but about business values,' Raju told his managers. And: 'We are not in the business of technology but in the business of building leaders.'

But clearly all this was not destined to succeed, because a part of Raju was clearly into a very local business – that of real estate. This part of his personality made him spend an inordinately long period of time in the offices of Maytas and direct his energies towards the business of these companies. Further, he inducted his sons into the Maytas business and kept them away from Satyam. 'At that time we thought that he was being professional – he wanted to keep Satyam as a corporate where the shareholders would enjoy dividends but professionals would run the company. But now we know that he had other things on his mind,' says a top manager of Satyam. Raju's elder son says that after he and his brother completed their education, the option of joining Satyam was not available to them; Raju wanted them to join Maytas.

It was not only his sons that Raju kept away from Satyam – he would often deflect highly qualified personnel, who would offer their services for the IT company, to Maytas. 'After working for many years abroad, I wanted to relocate to Hyderabad, my home town for family reasons. I was introduced to Raju and when I told him about wanting to work in Satyam, he said Maytas needs you. Satyam is a group company and you can join there later if you so desire,' says a former top Maytas executive. Adds a Satyam manager: 'In the last two to three years, we could visibly see that Raju's mind was moving away from Satyam. He was getting more focussed on Maytas and this was worrying us too.'

By his own admission, Raju had been misrepresenting his accounts for eight years before he made his dramatic confession. By that account Raju had become totally corrupt by 2001. But was he always like that? Or did he become dishonest on the way? A senior banker confides that D.V.S. Raju had once told Raju that it was quite impossible to work with him as his way of doing business was not easy to accept. Other analysts agree that Raju always had questionable ways of doing business; it's just that it came to public notice only recently. 'For instance, there was always a question mark on the amount of money that Satyam Infoway paid to acquire a clutch of websites after an ADR issue of the company. Was such a high amount paid or was some of it siphoned off? Nobody knows. But these questions were asked,' says a senior business analyst.

'I think greed got the better of Raju. He was certainly not a mean person, at least not in his personal dealings. But down the line he lost the sense of what is right or wrong. The Indian business culture is also partly to blame, as it is common for us to cut corners,' a corporate chief says. Raju's head began to turn when political bosses started lionizing him in their own interest. Raju suddenly realized that his standing, power and influence had increased and that he could get away with virtually anything. This feeling came after 2002, when the income tax department detected massive wrongdoing by him. But the politicians were close at hand to bail him out. Instead of punishing him, the income tax bosses transferred the officer who had exposed him. After this, uncontrollable greed seemingly became a part of Raju's psyche. But the world at large knew nothing of this because he was not given to talk much or make public statements.

'Raju continued to be soft-spoken, and strangely enough, his eyes – a window to the soul – reflected no evil or even a trace of arrogance or megalomania. So how would anybody have realized that he was up to mischief,' points out a senior Satyam staffer. In fact, his gentle look fooled many into thinking that Raju was monk-like. The fact that he was diplomatic and did not use harsh words only added to his aura. 'But obviously his diplomacy was of the cunning type and this is clear to us from his confession statement. The fact that he gave himself up has made some people say that he was a good man who made a mistake. I perceive that he did it to gain sympathy and in order to cover up a bigger crime – that is, swindling cash from the company,' says another senior manager of Satyam.

But the discerning ones were not taken in by Raju's ways. A businessman relates an incident when his senior and he had visited Raju to strike a business deal. 'Raju rambled on but never came to the point. He also made diagrams on a blackboard that he had kept in his drawing room. At the end of it, we were none the wiser. But when we came out, my colleague said, "Didn't you realize he was asking how much cut we would give him for the contract if he gave it to us?"' the businessman says. In other words, even while indulging in acts that were not exactly above board, Raju made every effort to ensure that he did not make anything obvious.

Some top corporate honchos might have had a faint idea about Raju's ways, but today they look back at him in amazement. 'He was obviously a genius, but an evil genius. To fudge books in an elaborate way for so many years and without any internal contradictions ever becoming public is something that required a high level of planning and sophistication. Add to this the money that he was allegedly siphoning off from the company. If only he had used his mind in a positive way, he would truly have ruled the world,' says a top IT baron. 'He was obviously very complicated, and only his wife or mother would have had an insight into his true personality,' says another industry baron.

How much did Raju's wife influence him? From all accounts, Nandini was not a bad influence on him at all. A traditional woman, Nandini kept to her home and as Raju became big, she took on social work. 'She's never been the flashy type, no Page 3 parties for her, though half of Hyderabad would have loved to invite her,' says a family associate who has known her. As Raju was immersed in his work, Nandini had complete control of the home. She even added a gym to the home, where Raju himself would work out. It was a happy joint family, and Raju's sons stayed with them for some time even after their marriage. Nandini was involved with an initiative called Alabama, which was aimed at giving computer training to underprivileged children. She was also part of the Crafts Council of Andhra Pradesh, as she had been interested in handicrafts ever since her childhood. In 2008, when Indus School decided to come to Hyderabad, the Rajus offered their land, and Nandini went on to become a part of the board of governors of the school.

In a sense, Nandini was always part of Raju's business plans because he held, bought and sold Satyam shares in her name. She was the director of many of Raju's privately owned companies that bought and sold land. She was also one of the two founder directors of the company set up to implement the Hyderabad metro rail project. But there is no evidence to suggest that she advised Raju on business affairs or that she had an inkling of the wrongdoings of her husband. In fact, Raju made a conscious decision to not discuss business matters with her. 'This is the typical pattern in a traditional family. Raju didn't tell her anything. Neither did she ask him any questions about business,' a family friend said.

More than his wife, it was his youngest brother who was a more important part of Raju's life. In Raju's world of business, it would be Rama Raju who would interpret for the world what Raju wanted. He would address communications to Satyam's staff and hold review meetings for senior Satyam managers. In negotiations, Raju would normally speak very little, but Rama would elaborate on the deal that Raju wanted. 'It was like a Ram-Lakshman jodi,' says somebody known to them for long. 'The relationship between the two was not equal. Rama was a more regular guy, and if he had not been under Raju's grip, he would not have fallen on these bad days. He just went along with Raju's plans,' says an old-time associate of Rama Raju. Rama was not a workaholic like his brother. 'In private he spoke quite a lot though in public he maintained an extremely low profile,' says a business associate who has seen the duo from close quarters. The importance of Rama in Raju's life can be gauged from the fact that he and his wife owned as many shares in Satyam as did Raju and Nandini. After 2007, however, there was some underlying friction between the two – probably to do with Raju actively pushing his sons into the business – but this never spilled out into the open.

Raju's sons were new-age kids brought up in Hyderabad. They had never stayed in the village and had grown up in prosperity. With a father like Raju, who was keen to leave them a substantial legacy, they had no reason to worry. Though not as modest as their father, the sons were well-behaved and did not throw their weight around. Neither were they seen partying and drinking in the Page 3 circuit. The elder son, Teja, was the more aggressive of the two but also more practical. But those who have worked with him say that he is yet to pick up the ropes of the business and is somewhat immature. Raju also realized this and had appointed Teja as merely the vice-chairman of Maytas Infra; a retired IAS official was the chairman, and a professional manager the chief executive officer.

Rama Jr was seen by their friends as more intelligent. He had a high score in GRE, an engineering degree from Carnegie Mellon, and an MBA from the Ross School of Business at the University of Michigan. 'There is nothing abnormal about the kids. They are crazy about cricket like anybody else of their age,' says a family friend. 'And they really looked up to their father and also to uncle Ramu.' Teja was up on social network sites like Facebook and boasted of 125 friends. He is said to be a fan of Sachin Tendulkar. Other than handling Maytas Infra and Maytas Properties, the two were also part of the private companies that Raju had established. Raju was proud of them, especially Teja. 'At a party, he once remarked that Teja had the potential of making as much money in a year as he had made in a lifetime,' says a top businessman who was present. Some close friends of the Rajus feel that Teja was the one who egged Raju on to foray deeper into land and often utilized the services of his mother for the purpose. 'She too was totally sold on the boy,' says a family friend.

No profile of Raju and his close associates can be complete without describing Srinivasa Vadlamani. Officially designated chief financial officer (CFO) and vice-president of Satyam, Vadlamani was a key operative of Raju without whose help the monumental fraud at Satyam could never have happened. For all his labours, Raju gave him taxable emoluments of Rs1.25 crore annually, which made him one of the highest paid executives of the company. 'This was a lot considering that he was really mediocre. Let me put it this way: if you collected twenty CFOs of top companies, Vadlamani would be the worst pick,' says a senior corporate executive in Hyderabad.

Vadlamani came from a modest rural background. After completing his M.Com from Osmania University, he joined Satyam as a senior manager in 1994. 'Vadlamani described himself as a servant who followed the orders of his bosses blindly and these are the qualities that brought him to Raju's notice. He was an important cog in Raju's scheme of things from 2001,' a senior Satyam employee reveals. Raju used the services of Vadlamani not only to fudge accounts but also to shield him from the outside world. Like Rama Raju, who would speak on behalf of the elder brother, Vadlamani handled financial institutions, stock markets and even the press on Raju's behalf. He would often be the interlocutor in press conferences, talking about the company's viewpoint even as Raju sat next to him.

Vadlamani was, however, a terror to the rest of his colleagues. 'He wielded extraordinary powers in Satyam. He could overrule anybody in the company and now we know why this was so,' the employee adds. Associates from Vadlamani's pre-Satyam days say that he was always unscrupulous. 'It is not that he got mesmerized by Raju and did everything. He was certainly taken in by the rewards that Raju gave him – in terms of bonus shares and rapid promotions. But he had no compunctions about the methods that he used to rise in life,' says an old associate of his. But from time to time, Vadlamani did have bouts of fear. He wondered who would bail him out if he was ever caught. Once, he did try to quit the company in a bid to wash his hands off the frauds being perpetrated by the Rajus. But he was too deeply involved in the scam, and the Raju brothers did not allow him to quit.

A few months before the scandal became public, Vadlamani started selling his shares in Satyam. On being asked about this vote of no confidence in the company that he worked for, Vadlamani said that he was building a house for himself and was therefore in need of ready cash. But like Raju, Vadlamani's external demeanour never betrayed his nervousness. 'Even after Raju and Ramu were behind bars, Vadlamani came to office and talked to us with a straight face. He seemed unaffected,' a Satyam manager says. However, he was later nabbed and sent to jail.

If Vadlamani was Raju's loyal servant, he also had a Man Friday – G. Ramakrishna, who was designated as vice-president of accounts. Presently cooling his heels in jail, he was not seen as mediocre by his peers. 'In a way, he was the man who ran Vadlamani and implemented the nefarious plans of the Raju brothers. He's the guy who thought of all the fudging techniques and actually put them into practice,' says one of his colleagues at Satyam. Like Vadlamani, he too was a terror within the company. 'In one instance, he refused to clear a bill. Even Raju could not overrule him,' a senior Satyam manager says.

Raju and his men ran a show that was scripted personally and with great care by the split personality that Raju was. For as long as it lasted it was great. But it was clearly not destined to last forever.

NINE

Crown Jewel of the Mahindras

It is rare to see two companies of the same vintage – but with very little in common – coming together to forge an intimate bond. The alliance between Satyam and Tech Mahindra falls in this category.

Tech Mahindra began its operations in 1987, the same year that Satyam started its business. Conceived as a joint venture between the Mahindra group and British Telecom, it started off as Mahindra-British Telecom. But in the early days there was nothing great about this company. Perhaps it was a difficult alliance between two partners with a dissimilar world view and culture, the net result being that the company just chugged along. In sharp contrast, Satyam had become a household name by 2000 and had almost reached the same league as Wipro, Infosys and Tata Consultancy Services. Few, apart from those in the information technology industry, knew anything about Mahindra-British Telecom. Possibly this was also because the domain of the company was limited: it was focussed on developing software for the telecom industry. Much of its business also came from a single client: British Telecom.

Things started brightening up in Mahindra-British Telecom only 2004 onwards, by which time the aggressive Anand Mahindra was at the helm of affairs. Earlier, the Mahindra empire was being looked after by his uncle, Keshub Mahindra. It was in 2006, when the company made an initial public offering (IPO), that it made rapid strides to break into the big boys' club. Simultaneous with the IPO, the company was renamed Tech Mahindra, the new identity being a kind of rebirth through which the company hoped to cater to a wider range of clients. By 2006, Satyam was already in the big league and Raju had started concentrating on the Maytas companies. Satyam had its IPO in 1992 and in 2006, Raju was mulling over the prospects of an IPO for Maytas Infra and Maytas Properties.

Under the stewardship of promoter Anand Mahindra and the able leadership of Vineet Nayyar, a former IAS officer of the Haryana cadre who later worked in the World Bank and was the chairman and managing director of the Gas Authority of India Limited (GAIL), Tech Mahindra became the sixth-largest IT company and the second-largest telecom software provider in India by 2008. But the company bosses were not satisfied. They were more aggressive than ever before and keen on expanding its operations.

The moment Satyam began to falter at the end of December 2008, Tech Mahindra started sending not-so-discreet feelers to Raju. So aggressive was the offensive that Raju, still the chairman of Satyam, sent a clarification on 6 January 2009 to the stock exchanges. There is no move to merge Satyam with Tech Mahindra, was the message. It was a day before Raju's confession, but he had not yet decided to exit. Vulnerable though he was, Raju was certainly in no mood to give up his empire to the Mahindras.

After Raju put in his papers and left the company in the hands of managers who did not fancy themselves as anything more than marketers of software, the Government of India moved in fast. Obtaining an order from the Company Law Board (CLB), the government appointed four eminent corporate persons on the board of Satyam to steer it out of the crisis. Thus, CII mentor Tarun Das, former Nasscom chief Kiran Karnik, HDFC chairman Deepak Parekh and corporate law expert V.S. Achutanandan entered the portals of Satyam's headquarters in Hyderabad's Infocity as the arbiters of its destiny. Later, two more directors – the well-known chartered accountant from Chennai, T.N. Manoharan, and LIC nominee S.B. Mainak – were also appointed.

It was a tough call for the new directors. Employees were looking for jobs even as clients called incessantly to find out if the contracts that they had awarded to Satyam would be executed at all. Those whose contracts were on the verge of completion had no intention of renewing them; some were even planning to take away the contracts midway. Clients would react to every press report about Satyam and get back to its battered managers with more queries. Often, competitor companies would slander Satyam and aggressively run it down, leading to more problems. Payments from clients also did not come on time. Morale was down and there was no money to pay even the salaries of employees. In fact, even a correct estimate of the staff strength of Satyam was not forthcoming. The story doing the rounds was that the company had a lot of dummy employees – fictitious salary rolls had been created to siphon off money from Satyam by the Rajus. What compounded problems was that there was no authentic data about the company. A company's assets, liabilities, profits, losses and other financial data are laid out in its books of accounts. But in the case of Satyam, it was all a lie. Even the money lying in the accounts of Satyam was fictitious and did not exist. Many of the invoices found in the records were also falsely created. To add to the confusion, enforcement and other investigating agencies arrived in hordes at the Satyam office following unprecedented reactions from the public.

There was another major obstacle that the directors faced: they did not know how many of the top officials of Satyam were complicit with Raju. The problem was that even if some of the top managers had collaborated with Raju, they were also the ones who knew about the state of affairs in the company. So, not taking their help would be a limiting factor.

Even as the new directors were trying hard to fix a new line of credit for Satyam to help it tide over its financial crisis, A.M. Naik, chairman of Larsen & Toubro (L&T), one of the largest business conglomerates in India, announced his intent to bid for Satyam. L&T had an infotech unit that operated as a subsidiary of the parent company, but with just 12,800 employees, it was certainly not in the big league. Naik, under whom L&T had aggressively pursued growth, was looking for new IT acquisitions and had, in fact, set apart a budget for shopping. On 23 January, L&T informed the bourses that it now owned 12.04 per cent of the shares of Satyam. It had picked up 7.56 per cent of the company's shares in the past few days, in addition to the 4.48 per cent that L&T already possessed. Naik was seen in the corridors of power in New Delhi, and it was clear that he wanted a board seat for an L&T representative, pending the negotiations of takeover of the company. B.K. Modi of the Spice Group also threw his hat in the ring and wrote to the Satyam board about his desire to acquire the company.

Whatever might have been the discussions that Naik had with high government officials and ministers, the powers that be were not inclined to hand over Satyam to L&T on a platter. The new board raised Rs 600 crore for the working capital needs of Satyam by assiduously courting banks and appointed an old Raju crony, A.S. Murthy, as the CEO. This left analysts dumbfounded, but the choice fell on him possibly because of his deep knowledge of the state of affairs in the company.

The government represented to the CLB that the financial crunch in Satyam was so severe that it would require a knight in shining armour, a strategic investor, to pump in money and provide managerial expertise. Only such a move could rescue Satyam. But a strategic investor should be chosen through a global competitive bid, the government had represented. This was obviously to stave off any allegation of favouritism that might be levelled if the company was given away through negotiations.

Since the scrip of Satyam had tanked and was quoted at a measly Rs 20 per share, it was decided to raise the authorized share capital of Satyam from Rs 160 to 280 crore. The government also decided that the number of shares of the company (of Rs 2 par value) would be increased from 80 crore to 140 crore. A part of these increased shares (that would total 31 per cent of the equity of Satyam) could be allotted to a strategic investor on a preferential basis. But at what price would the allotment be made? That was the more crucial point and it was decided that the price would be determined through bids. To ensure transparency in the process, the services of a former chief justice of India, S.P. Bharucha, were requisitioned for overseeing the selection process. After getting 31 per cent of the shares of Satyam, the successful bidder would also have to make an open offer and acquire 20 per cent of Satyam's equity from the market at the price at which they get the preferential allotment. This was as per the takeover guidelines in the country.

In the event, Tech Mahindra's desire to align with Satyam seemed to be much more than that of L&T. So while Tech Mahindra quoted an outlandish (or so it seemed then) price of

Rs 58 per share, L&T offered a more modest Rs 45.90 per share. There was a third bidder too: a consortium of private equity funds led by W.L. Ross. But they quoted abysmally low at Rs 20 per share. Though the new directors had shared a document regarding Satyam's performance, the information was still not authentic, and L&T decided not to go all out. The document shared with bidders suggested that for the quarter ending 31 December 2008, Satyam had a turnover of Rs 2,206 crore and a profit of Rs 181 crore. In January 2009, the worst month for the company, Satyam did a business of Rs 647 crore and made Rs 4 crore after paying taxes. But in February, this went up to Rs 676 crore and profits after tax jumped to Rs 52 crore. The document, however, warned that the figures, though consolidated from internal company documents, were based on a lot of assumptions and presumptions. This implied that they could turn out to be wrong at a later stage. But the document also revealed that till 26 March, a total of sixty-six contracts valued at $183 million had been cancelled. At the same time, 215 new contracts valued at $380 million had been signed up.

Apparently, the bullish Naik was not ready to stick his neck out to bid high for a company which, apart from its other problems, was also likely to have lawsuits filed against it in the US. These lawsuits could result in a substantial outgo from Satyam in terms of fines and penalties. As a consequence, the new owner could be badly scalded. The above-mentioned document gave details of these lawsuits (and potential ones) that made claims of about Rs 6,500 crore from Satyam. This included claims of Rs 5,000 crore by Upaid, which had charged Satyam with selling off patent rights that rightly belonged to them and claims of Rs 1,230 crore from Raju's private companies.

Globally, W.L. Ross, a leading turnaround group, is known to be a buyer of distressed assets. The group's low quote was based on its valuation of Satyam as a distressed asset. A disincentive for the group was the condition that the new stakeholder could not sell its shares for three years. The group probably did not have full confidence that Satyam could be made to stand on its feet in a short period. But if it got Satyam cheaply, it could make money by virtue of getting the asset at a rock bottom price. Additionally, IT major Cognizant Technology, which was supposed to be part of W.L. Ross's bid, withdrew at the last minute, giving jitters to the turnaround experts. The Hindujas, who were expected to bid, also withdrew.

Perhaps it was Satyam's fate to be allied with Tech Mahindra. It was 13 April, barely a hundred days after Raju had written his confession, when the orphaned Satyam's adoption was finalized. In some ways, it was a quirk of destiny that Satyam, supposedly with a headcount of 53,000 and operating from sixty-six countries in its heyday, had been taken over by Tech Mahindra that had 25,000 employees and operated from just fourteen countries. Tech Mahindra had purchased Satyam's shares for Rs 1,756 crore. It had to acquire another 20 per cent through a public offer at the same price. This would raise the total cost of acquisition to Rs 2,889 crore.

Howsoever benevolent an orphan's adopter might be, it is not easy to adjust to life with a foster parent. Satyam's employees, pampered for too long by Ramalinga Raju, realized this quickly. Tech Mahindra closed down offices that it thought were not necessary and began an exercise of scorching cost-cutting. It also brought in chosen executives from Tech Mahindra to preside over the destiny of Satyam. This included a chief executive officer, a chief financial officer, and a chief operating officer. A.S. Murthy, who had been appointed by the government as CEO, was moved to a lower position. A board comprising top executives from Tech Mahindra was also established.

By the time Tech Mahindra took it over, Satyam had 38,000 employees. But within weeks of entering Satyam, the new owners unleashed what is called a virtual pool programme (VPP). This is a thinly disguised scheme to get rid of staff. Under this scheme, 7,000 to 10,000 associates of Satyam, who are in non-billable roles for three months or more, are sent home. For six months, they will be paid part of their salary: the basic salary, provident fund and medical insurance. If the business of Satyam improves by then or there are new jobs in the company for these associates, they will be recalled. Otherwise, these associates will have to bid goodbye. Incidentally, most of those who are in non-billable roles are support services staff, but they do include techies. Though Tech Mahindra managers adorn the top posts in Satyam, their numbers are not large enough nor have they penetrated the company deeply. So the job of identifying the excess associates had been given to existing departmental heads. If stories doing the rounds are correct, a fair job has not been done in every case. There are charges of gross favouritism and that seniors have saved their jobs and sacrificed juniors.

A glimpse of what lay ahead for Satyam was also on view at the end of June 2009 when its brand name was changed to Mahindra-Satyam. A new logo has also been designed and the website of Satyam has been recast. Tech Mahindra bosses have also indicated that at an appropriate time – and after approval of shareholders and registrar of companies – Satyam's name will also be changed (so far only the brand name used in advertising and logos has been changed to 'Mahindra Satyam'). It is also likely that Satyam might, at a later stage, be merged with Tech Mahindra, and by present estimates this might be sooner them expected. This is exactly what the Tech Mahindra bosses had wanted to do in Raju's last days.

But as Tech Mahindra entrenches itself further and the government-appointed directors of Satyam bid goodbye, the surviving employees of Satyam are quite happy. As one of the survivors says: 'It was a difficult choice. It was a question of saving jobs. If 7,000 to 10,000 jobs are lost to save the remaining 28,000 jobs, I think that is a better course to adopt.' The consensus is that Tech Mahindra has got Satyam cheaply. Proof of this lies in the fact that the shares of Satyam jumped in the aftermath of the takeover. The Rs 58 per share offered by Satyam looked high at the time the bids opened, but within weeks, the company's scrip jumped to Rs 80. This, in fact, is now proving to be an obstacle for Tech Mahindra. As per law, Tech Mahindra has offered to buy shares from the public at Rs 58 per share. But with the market prices ruling at a much higher level, who will sell shares to them at this lower price? Now it seems that Tech Mahindra will have to be content running Satyam with a lower equity holding of around 44 per cent. However, that scarcely matters as Raju ran Satyam with 8.5 per cent shares for over a decade.

While taking over Satyam, Tech Mahindra also inherited the land bank of 450 acres that Raju's former company possessed in the technology centre and Infocity campuses in Hyderabad. Fifty per cent of the land is freehold and the entire land bank is valued at Rs 1,700 crore. Satyam is expected to add $1 billion (nearly Rs 5,000 crore) annually to Tech Mahindra's revenues. This will push the company to the big league and place it alongside Tata Consultancy Services (TCS), Infosys and Wipro. The telecom company's domain expertise will also broaden – it will get an entry into the BFIS (banking, financial services, insurance segment), where Satyam has its core expertise. This will enable the company to pitch more aggressively for various projects.

Satyam is now truly the jewel in the Tech Mahindra crown. In the software business, a company's assets are its manpower, contracts and brand name. That Satyam's crisis coincided with the global financial meltdown meant that not all the staff who wanted to leave could do so. Also, not many clients of Satyam left – many of them were midway through their contracts and could not leave suddenly and this also helped Tech Mahindra. Satyam's prices were low, which meant that clients were getting their work done cheaply. They did not want to shift to a more costly option. There is also a view that the legal suits against Satyam will not result in much damage, and again this is because of the bad times. Surveys show that lawsuits in US are less during a slowdown, and in any case over 90 per cent of these disputes are settled out of court.

Personnel from two leading audit companies, KPMG and Deloitte, are now toiling day and night to compile the books of Satyam and restate its accounts for the last three years. This is a daunting task and expected to be complete only by the end of 2009. The new bosses of Satyam are also working at a furious pace and their top managers, led by Vineet Nayyar, have started travelling the world scouring for more business. Other measures for rectifying the state of affairs are also being taken. The new owners have written to the World Bank seeking a revocation of the eight-year ban imposed by the multilateral agency for awarding contracts to Satyam.

Looking back, it seems quite a feat that the distressed asset that Satyam was when Raju left could be rehabilitated in less than six months. This will probably go some way in helping the Indian corporate sector recover from the shock of the Satyam scam. 'Across the world, in the aftermath of the Raju episode, corporate governance norms in India came to be questioned. But with Satyam getting rehabilitated so soon, the other side of the coin is also on display,' says Harish Chandra Prasad, president of the Hyderabad chapter of CII. At the same time, there is

.one conclusion that is inescapable. In their bid to rehabilitate Satyam, these directors did nothing to identify the guilty men of the company. There were many top managers in Satyam who had more than a clue about what was going on in the company. They are guilty of being accomplices in Raju's nefarious designs. Possibly, the directors left it to the law enforcement agencies to identify the wrongdoers. The new owners of Satyam have their task cut out. With the mess that the company's accounts are in, the all-pervading confusion pertaining to its rolls, the issues of building credibility and trust all over again, Mahindra–Satyam might just realize that the acquisition was the easy part. The real battle lies ahead.

TEN

The End of the Road

Possibly reflecting the inner yearning of the inmates, Independence Day is celebrated with gusto in Indian jails. But this time around, when the tricolour was hoisted in the precincts of Hyderabad's Chanchalguda jail on 15 August 2009, the Raju brothers were conspicuous by their absence, though they had not sought leave of absence from the jail authorities. Given their superior social status even in jail, the authorities are unlikely to pull up the Rajus for their absence, which they attribute to the desire of the former Satyam boss to keep away from the *aam janata*. Yes, even in jail, the Rajus seem to be living by their own rules.

Once in ten days or so, Raju's wife, Nandini, comes to meet him and once a week Raju's lawyer, Bharat Kumar, sees his client. Because of his educational qualifications and his previous lifestyle, the jail authorities have allowed Raju 'B'-class facilities. This allows him proper food: non-vegetarian dishes of his choice

– chicken, mutton or fish – every day. He even has a cook to whip up his meals and has help to clean his cell and wash his clothes. These are drawn from prisoners who are serving terms of rigorous imprisonment. However, at times Raju's brother boils the rice. Raju himself hasn't ever been in the kitchen all his life, and so he has no culinary skills.

Now that Satyam has slipped out of his hand, Raju has plenty of time to think about how to save the Maytas empire for his sons and protect the land owned by his extended family. He also reads books on science fiction and metaphysics. Occasionally he asks for comics too. They act as stress busters. His health is not particularly good, but he has refrained from seeking a remand to the hospital. To reduce tension, the normally workaholic Raju has taken to playing outdoor games like badminton. A special court has been laid for the benefit of the Raju brothers. Jail officials say that 'B'-class undertrials are entitled to such facilities and that there is a provision for laying badminton/basketball courts – it is just that nobody had asked for them in the past.

Even if you have money, jail life in India can be difficult if there is nobody to guide you about the ways there. But Raju has been singularly lucky in meeting a scamster like Venkateshwar Rao behind bars. Rao, who used to run a bank called Krishi Bank, had fled to Thailand after swindling it but, three years ago, was extradited back. Since then, he has been in Chanchalguda and is now guiding Raju about how things work in jail. He also often prepares a curry or two for the brothers. It seems that the health-conscious Raju is fond of his cooking because he uses less spices and oil. Raju has also earned some admirers in jail – including jail officials – because he has been doling out advice on how to invest in stock markets.

The investigations by the CBI are still not complete, although the agency filed its charge sheet in the first week of April, just

ahead of the statutory limitation period of three months. A
supplementary charge sheet will be filed later after the agency is
able to take the investigations to their logical conclusion. That's
going to be a tough job because it would require a close look
at the overseas operations of Satyam. The multidisciplinary CBI
team – comprising not only policemen but also financial sleuths
adept at reading balance sheets and IT wizards well-versed with
computer systems – has realized that it will not be able to crack
the case all by itself. It has now requested help from the Interpol
and has requisitioned the services of the Enforcement Directorate.
In the meantime, the CBI has also obtained permission from the
Andhra Pradesh High Court to set up a special court for a fast
trial – in regular courts the process would take years. Lawyers
believe that if the case as it stands is proven, Raju may be in jail
for at least ten years.

However, the first chargesheet does not inspire much
confidence that Raju will be nailed comprehensively. Hampered
by the fact that the case was handled by the Andhra Pradesh
police's CID for nearly two months, the CBI has fashioned a
charge sheet that mainly reproduces Raju's confession statement.
In other words, the CBI will depend on Raju's confession to
nail him for fudging the books of Satyam and inflating the
company's income and profits. How far this will succeed
cannot be predicted, because in the trial court Raju can retract
his statements, claiming that he was under some kind of mental
duress when he went public with his confession. Raju has been
charged under sections 120B, 420, 467, 468, 471, 477A and
201 of the Indian Penal Code (IPC). Broadly speaking, these
sections relate to cheating and hatching a criminal conspiracy
to cheat.

The CBI now asserts that it is well on its way to nail Raju for
pilfering cash from Satyam and book him under other sections

of the IPC (which it has not yet specified). However, as it stands, the charge sheet is unable to prove that the Rajus pilfered cash.

Also interesting is the fact that instead of registering multiple complaints, the CBI is depending on the complaint filed against Raju by a retired bank official, Leena Mangat. The Andhra Pradesh police had already taken cognizance of this. Mangat had invested money in the shares of Satyam and when the share prices collapsed in the wake of Raju's confession, she suffered pecuniary losses. Lawyers say that the prosecution agencies always get more than one complaint registered in a case with such vast ramifications. It then becomes easier to fix the offender. Multiple complaints registered under different sections of law also prove handy in denying bail to the accused. Why the agency did not have more complaints registered is not clear.

While presenting the first charge sheet, the CBI brought a truckload of documents, which have now been placed in the court registery. Going through so many documents will be a major problem for the judge. However, the CBI may not be the only agency probing the Satyam scam. With Satyam being listed on the New York Stock Exchange, numerous 'class action suits' have been filed by American shareholders in the courts there. All of them relate to losses to investors because the value of Satyam scrip fell after Raju confessed. As a result of these class action suits, the Securities Exchange Commission (SEC) – the US corporate watchdog body – has swung into action. A team from SEC has been visiting India off and on. In the course of their visits they have had meetings with the CBI and the new owners of Satyam. The SEC, of course, is probing only the Satyam angle of the Raju fraud. In their meetings with the new bosses of Satyam, SEC officials have been told that they would have to wait a few months till the restatement of the company's accounts. Only after that will it be known precisely how much money has been swindled. But preliminary indications are that the SEC may not be willing to wait so long.

On its part, the SEC has done a bit of digging around in the US to verify whether all the clients Satyam claimed it had actually existed. The US agencies have also possibly accessed the bank accounts of Satyam in that country to figure out the nature of transactions there. As per the usual practice, if there is a serious offence registered against Raju in the US and the authorities there so demand, he can be extradited there after completion of trial in India. Extradition can, however, happen only after proper legal procedures, which means that both the US and Indian courts have to allow it.

Till the end of June 2009, Raju's bail plea has been rejected six times. In five instances, he applied for bail to the metropolitan court in Hyderabad. It is only in the last instance that the bail plea was made in the high court. It is believed that the former Satyam boss does not really intend to get out on bail so fast. If he had really wanted bail, he would have knocked at every door, including the Supreme Court. Raju knows well that there's trouble waiting for him outside. 'He has borrowed money and the lenders will be at his throat the moment he gets out,' say people who claim to know him. Raju, of course, has land, but he cannot sell it off to pay his creditors. Land prices are still depressed and if the real estate market had been good, Raju would anyway not have gone to jail. He would have sold parts of the land and generated enough cash to stave off trouble.

Raju's lawyers have thwarted efforts by the cops to put him through a lie detector test, claiming that he was cooperating fully with the investigators and that there was no need for such a test. But now the courts have agreed to the police plea. So Raju, Rama and Vadlamani will have their brains mapped and will be subjected to a polygraph test to ascertain whether they are lying. The test will, however, be conducted in the presence of the lawyers and the trio will have to be flown all the way to a forensic lab in Ahmedabad. Raju's lawyers have also made every possible effort to keep away SFIO, SEBI and Enforcement Directorate officials from interrogating him in jail. They did not ultimately succeed, but the lawyers were able to postpone such custodial questioning. It is doubtful if these agencies were able to get anything out of him. Raju is measured in what he says and in the presence of the interrogators he is reported to have become even more reticent.

Raju has been uncooperative since the day he surrendered on 9 January 2009. After negotiating with his police sources, Raju arrived at 10 p.m. at the head of a cavalcade. Post a midnight session that included a check-up by a doctor of Raju's choice (usually the police bring in a government doctor), the CID sleuths, after obtaining orders from a magistrate, shifted him to their office. The visit to the magistrate's house was not without drama – traffic had to be controlled on the roads to keep away bystanders who had queued up.

In custody, the CID plied Raju with good food brought from hotels, and questioned him only between 10 a.m. to 5 p.m. in the presence of his lawyers. But Raju would not reveal anything more than what he had confessed in his letter. He took long to answer even simple questions put to him. In one instance, he took over one hour to answer a question. The police were helpless, trained as they are in third-degree methods, which they obviously could not use on him. A senior police official monitored the interrogation on close circuit TV, as his junior posed questions to Raju. The senior sent his questions on a piece of paper to the junior, if he had to ask any supplementaries. Why the senior official did not confront Raju directly is a mystery.

The police, however, progressed in their investigations by talking to other persons related to Raju's land dealings and other Satyam staffers whom they summoned for long sessions but did not finally arrest. A flat used to store documents pertaining to Raju's transactions was discovered in the Punjagutta area of Hyderabad. Painstakingly working through documents in the various offices of the stamps and registrations department, records of land owned by the Raju family were unearthed. Properties held under various names in the Raju enclave in the Medchal area of Hyderabad were also discovered. Raju's distant relative, D. Gopalakrishnan Raju, who acted as the general manager of SRSR Advisory Services, was of invaluable help to the cops. Though arrested and later released on bail, Gopalakrishnan has not been chargesheeted. Suryanarayana absconded soon after Raju gave himself up. A few weeks later – on 7 March, almost two months after Raju was arrested – he surrendered but is now out on bail. He has been slapped with a smaller number of sections of the IPC than Raju and Rama.

Whether Raju gets bail, whether he is proven guilty, whether he gets a life term, in the public mind he is guilty. Many people do not know the intricacies of the case but they know that what Raju did is unacceptable. Of course, public memory is short in India and it is possible that Raju may be rehabilitated in the eyes of the public in the future.

As for Satyam's employees, their initial disbelief and shock gave way to anger, then a sense of resignation and ultimately an acceptance. Illustrative of this, in the last week of June 2009, there was a meeting of Satyam employees in the company's training and conferencing facility at Bahadurpally in Hyderabad. The meeting had been convened by the new promoters of Satyam and in the course of the deliberations, there was a discussion about whether the photos of Raju that adorned the walls of the facility should be allowed to remain. Some employees said that they should be torn down but most others insisted that Raju's pictures should stay. Although not at the helm any more, he had built the company and therefore was a central part of its history.

For the women in the Raju clan, the events after 7 January came as a bolt from the blue. In a traditional feudal set-up, the women are not empowered, and are just appendages of their men. Thus, in the Raju household, business was never discussed at home and although assets were registered in the name of these women, they merely affixed their signatures where they were asked to. Immersed in social work, Raju's wife never knew what her husband was up to. This realization has now dawned on Nandini and with devastating effect. From a lady much sought after in social circles, she has become an outcaste. Soon after the Satyam scam broke out, Nandini was requested to step down from the governing council of the Indus School, which stands on land given out by the Rajus, and her name was removed from the school's website. To provide moral support to her daughter, Nandini's mother has moved in from her village. Her father had earlier also moved into the Raju household. But, unable to bear the eerie silence and the mournful atmosphere, he went back to the village.

The mental anguish of Radha is believed to be worse. According to knowledgeable sources, she has all but totally broken down. Her parents, who stay in Hyderabad, are planning to shift back to their ancestral village to find their own peace. 'The women in the family have really been hit badly. Dad and uncle are okay and can take care of themselves. But these ladies require looking after,' says Teja Raju.

Ramalinga Raju realized that even if his wife could bear the agony of seeing her husband in jail, his mother would not be able to withstand the shock. Appalanarasamma, nearing eighty, lives alone in a house in the Raju enclave in Hyderabad. Of course, she has servants and family retainers to take care of her. In what would seem a scene straight out of a teleserial, she has not been told that her sons are in jail. She believes that they have gone abroad on a long assignment. The members of the extended family, who once basked in Raju's glory, are now feeling the heat and have become objects of ridicule. Many of them have started selling off their properties and are moving on.

The lone man standing in the Raju family is Teja Raju, who can be spotted off and on in Delhi and Mumbai. He tried hard to save the Maytas empire by trying to rope in investors to bail out his company. He was not averse to inducting a strategic investor and even selling off the company. But in the end he failed. He was kicked out before he found a partner.

Though the focus of investigating agencies is on Satyam, Maytas Infra and Maytas Properties are also under the scanner. Officials from the Registrar of Companies, Serious Fraud Investigations Office and other agencies have been asking for the records of the two companies. The latest indication is that the RoC has figured out that a part of the proceeds of realization from the public issue of Maytas Infra in 2007 was diverted to family firms of the Rajus. But Ved Jain, a government-appointed director of the board of Maytas Infra and Maytas Properties (government directors were appointed to ensure that the company ran as per the laws of the land), has publicly claimed that the money diverted from the company went to the coffers of Satyam through a clutch of transactions. 'A sum of Rs 380 crore from Maytas Infra and Rs 220 crore from Maytas Properties – totalling Rs 600 crore – entered the accounts of Satyam and we have papers to prove that. We shall soon ask for the return of the money from Satyam,' Ved Jain has been quoted as saying. However, Vineet Nayyar, the new boss of Satyam, is not amused. He in turn has said that there was no question of Satyam paying back money, because there was nothing in the internal records of the company to show that any funds came into its coffers from either Maytas Infra or Maytas Properties.

Meanwhile, many projects of Maytas Infra have already been cancelled. These include the Rs 12,200-crore project for the Hyderabad metro rail, which was responsible for landing Raju in a soup. The government terminated the project after Maytas was unable to pay the performance guarantee, despite being given repeated extensions of up to six months. The government has also forfeited the Rs 71 crore that Maytas paid initially.

Maytas has now gone to the high court to challenge the cancellation of the contract. Their contention: Satyam and Maytas are different agencies but the latter got tarred by the same brush as the former by banks, financial institutions and others. As a result, it would be reasonable to say that Maytas got affected by factors beyond its control. This is the reason why Maytas could not pay the performance guarantee and therefore, the contract should not be cancelled.

But all this is now the headache of Infrastructure Leasing & Financial Services Limited (IL&FS), the new promoter of Maytas. A joint venture of Central Bank Of India, HDFC and Unit Trust of India, the company is in the business of catalyzing the development of infrastructure in the country. IL&FS had earlier lent money to the Rajus against shares of Maytas pledged by them. When the Rajus failed to repay their loan, the shares became the property of IL&FS. Finding this, CLB handed over Maytas to them and anointed the company as the new promoter.

Contracts for modernizing two airports in Karnataka that had come Maytas's way were first cancelled and then restored to the company. High-level lobbying involving top politicians of different parties was instrumental in this restoration. Faced with a financial crunch, Maytas Infra has also experienced difficulty in paying salaries to staff. As a result, a large number of them have left. The chairman of Maytas Infra, R.C. Sinha, a retired IAS officer, left the company in the aftermath of the Satyam episode and so did some directors. The extent of the financial crunch can be gauged from the fact that the company did not have revenue of a single paisa in the three months after the Satyam scam broke. On the other hand, its costs mounted what with heavy machinery and other equipment hired for contracts standing idle and unutilized.

Like Satyam, Maytas was unable to finalize its accounts for the financial year ending March 2009 for long. At the end of five months it showed a loss of Rs 490 crore. It is estimated to have incurred losses of Rs 75 crore every month for six months after the Satyam scam was exposed. The huge losses were not surprising because the company had a huge outgo in the form of fixed charges like interest on sums borrowed, lease rentals on equipment engaged etc., while there was no income. To compound problems for Maytas, many banks, such as HSBC, which had given loans to Raju, have started recalling them. In the first half of July, however, the government-appointed directors on the board of Maytas were able to wrangle a loan of Rs 350 crore from banks to keep the company afloat. Four government nominees, including a chairman, were appointed on the board of Maytas Infra in February 2009. This happened after the government moved the Company Law Board wanting to supersede Maytas's board of directors and taking over the management, as in the case of Satyam. The CLB did not agree to the government plea of taking over the management and instead allowed the appointment of four directors on the board of Maytas Infra and one on the board of Maytas Properties. This plea was ultimately upheld by the CLB on 31 August 2009.

The situation is worse in Maytas Properties. A criminal case has been filed against Rama Raju (junior) by irritated customers who are accusing him of cheating and reneging on promises. These customers had booked fancy villas and bungalows that Maytas Properties promised to deliver in its Maytas Hill County project and had paid large sums as deposits (some had paid over Rs 50 lakhs to the company). But now the company is unable to proceed further on the projects and is seeking more money from those who have booked the houses.

The customers are in a fix: if they don't pay up, the houses will not be completed and if they pay they still don't know whether Maytas Properties will be in a position to go forward. Belonging to the upper crust of society many of those who booked houses initially preferred to solve their problems behind closed doors. But a few months later, in July 2009, realizing that nothing would be achieved without creating a shindig, they took to the streets. Demonstrating outside Raju's residence, they demanded their money back and appealed to the government to intervene. A delegation had gone and met the late Andhra Pradesh chief minister, Rajasekhara Reddy, who told them that he could do nothing but suggested that they file a complaint. The hint was taken and a complaint filed. But Teja Raju is unfazed. 'If my brother is able to execute the Maytas Hill County project – which I am sure he will manage – then things are bright,' he says. Maytas Properties is locked in a dispute with India Infinity Investment Funds, which had invested Rs 600 crore in the company. Meanwhile, nearly 90 per cent of the staff of Maytas Properties has been forced to resign amidst protests and the company has virtually folded up.

The appointment of government directors on the board of the two Maytas firms had initially helped Teja Raju greatly.

The four directors of Maytas Infra, including the government-appointed chairman of the company, worked zealously as per their mandate to revive the company. Although the CLB move to appoint government directors was to help the shareholders of the company, the fact is that a large percentage of the equity of Maytas Infra was owned by Raju's cronies. In effect, these public directors were furthering the Raju cause. However, the directors soon discovered that investigative agencies were hot on the company's trail for giving out unsecured loans (not backed by collaterals) to the Rajus' private companies.

One organization whose reputation seems to have taken a serious knock, post-Satyam, is the auditing firm, Pricewaterhouse-Coopers (PwC), which had done the statutory audit of the Raju company. When Raju first confessed, many people thought that he must have hoodwinked the auditors. At most, the auditors were guilty of omission, of being lax in their work, was the general impression. But within a few days, the police arrested two partners – S. Gopalakrishnan and Srinivas Talluri – from the Hyderabad office of PwC, and suggested that the two were guilty of acts of commission. According to the charge sheet filed with the court, the two were fully complicit with Raju and had full knowledge of what was happening. They knew that Satyam's books of accounts were fudged and that the figures projected in the balance sheet were also false. They were part of the conspiracy and deliberately certified the wrong figures, it is being alleged.

To start with, PwC vigorously defended its two auditors. In the last week of June, the chairman and CEO of PwC India, Ramesh Rajan, was called by the CBI for questioning. The CEO said that the auditing of the Satyam accounts, though carried out by Gopalakrishnan and Talluri, had been done by another audit firm, Lovelock and Lewes (L & L). Although L & L was part of the network of PwC, since the tainted auditors had done their work through L & L, they were not entitled to sign the audit reports on behalf of PwC.

Though Raju has been relatively calm and composed in jail, the auditors – especially Gopalakrishnan – seem to be rather impatient. A central council member of the Institute of Chartered Accountants of India (ICAI), whose name had been bandied around in an earlier financial scam concerning the Global Trust Bank Bank and who is perceived as some kind of a dada by the Hyderabad chartered accountant fraternity, Gopalakrishnan has moved the court as many as seventeen times for bail. But all his pleas have been unsuccessful. Not surprising, considering it has now been found that even an internal team of PwC, which does a check to see whether their company's auditors are doing a thorough job, had reported serious deficiencies in the work being done for Satyam.

Unquestioning loyalty and blind obedience of the boss is part of the Indian corporate culture. But for two relatively junior managers in Raju's establishment, Venkatapathy Raju and Ch Srisailam, doing so has led to disaster. They were part of the finance department where the fraud was being executed. They would have surely realized that what they were doing was immoral, if not illegal, but where was the question of their saying no? They were being rewarded for this in the form of employee stock options. They felt that they were part of an exclusive club in the top-ranking company. This swelled their ego and self-esteem and they agreed to do anything asked of them. In fact, they felt proud to be the chosen ones. Venkatapathy, being from the Raju community, was also Raju's country cousin and the services of his wife had been requisitioned for selling off Satyam shares belonging to the Raju family in 2000. Now, the chickens have come home to roost for the two. Both are cooling their heels in jail, charged with the same sections that the Raju brothers have been. They run the prospect of being sentenced to the same term as their super boss. Also keeping them company in jail is G. Ramakrishna, their immediate boss. After he seemed to have confessed all that he did to the police, there was the possibility that he could become an approver in the case. But a day before the charge sheet was filed, he was put behind bars and also charged with offences of hatching conspiracy and cheating people. A vice-president of accounts, Ramakrishna was the link between Vadlamani and these junior managers.

Raju's confession and arrest came on the eve of Sankranti, the biggest festival in Andhra Pradesh held to mark the entry of Sun into Capricorn on 13 January. This is a festival celebrated with great fervour by Raju's clansmen. Every year, taking time off his busy schedule, Raju would spend a few days in his native village during the time of Sankranti. But this time the celebrations were suspended and Raju's clansmen went into mourning. Most of them felt that Raju had done nothing wrong. Demonstrations were held in Raju's village and those loyal to him performed havans and offered pujas in temples. Many of these community members, who had invested heavily in Satyam shares, also lost financially due to the falling value of the scrip. But they did not seem to mind: for them, Raju's welfare was the most important thing.

But in these last few months, a lot of water has passed through the rivers Krishna and Godavari. The extreme sympathy that Raju evoked among his clansmen living in the Raju enclave is now a thing of the past. Most of them are indifferent to his plight and many have turned against him. They feel that Ramalinga has done a great disservice to the community, since the Raju surname now raises eyebrows every time it is mentioned in the public. These people have begun to believe that Raju and Rama were not as innocent as they posed; and with more evidence emerging, many of them are convinced that Raju really meant to cheat. A part of the discomfiture of Raju's clansmen in Hyderabad is also because of the constant visits by the police to their enclave. Back in his native district, the community is upset because most of the development work undertaken by the Byrraju Foundation has come to a standstill.

What is Raju's own take on Satyam gate? Being in jail, he is not accessible. His lawyer, Bharat Kumar, says that whatever his client has to say will be before the judge in the trial court. According to him, as stated in Raju's confessional letter, Raju had inflated his revenues and profits only to save Satyam. 'There is nothing more to it,' he says with force.

Teja says, 'Believe me. Not that he had shared this with us, but Satyam could have become the target of a takeover. He did all this to save the company, for the sake of the 50,000 employees who worked in the company,' he adds. In effect, if Raju had not confessed, in these six months the company would have disintegrated because there was no cash in the company.

Not many believe Raju's version but experts feel that he could well go back on his confession in the trial court. He might come up with an entirely different story. Six months in jail is enough to fix your defences and make them impregnable. Raju confessed in a hurry, but will fight his case with élan, say those who know him closely.

The Raju story is, however, far from over. Every new day brings forth a new revelation. For instance, in the first week of August 2009, news of trouble – of a political nature – came from Victoria state in Australia. The allegation was that the state government had paid unspecified amounts and allotted free land to Satyam in April 2008 to establish software units in a town close to Melbourne. While taking the money (the amount has not yet been made public), Raju promised 2,000 jobs, but never showed up again.

The Enforcement Directorate has now found evidence that the Rajus had bought 287 properties in Hyderabad, Chennai, Bangalore and Nagpur using the scam-tainted money from Satyam. The properties were bought in the name of eighty front companies between 2005-09 and include Teja Raju's residence (built on 4000 square feet of land) in Jubilee Hills in Hyderabad. The value of the properties is conservatively estimated at Rs 5,000 crores. In mid-August, invoking the provisions of the Prevention of Money Laundering Act, the Enforcement Directorate attached the properties, though they have not seized them yet. The Rajus can't mortgage or sell these properties now, and will be tried separately for violating the provisions of the money-laundering act.

Ramalinga Raju was a clever operator who played his cards close to his chest. Unless he himself decides to tell his own story, the world will never know the full extent of his machinations. In one of his last known interviews, given to a society magazine barely a month and a half before his confession, Raju was asked whether he could gaze into the crystal ball and predict what he would be doing in future. His answer was almost prophetic: 'I see myself engaged less in operational work and more in reading or researching.'

That's what he was doing in jail until 7 September 2009, when he was rushed to Nizam's Institute of Medical Science (NIMS) in Hyderabad after a mild heart attack. However, that's not the only ailment plaguing Raju. He has had a relapse of a liver infection that he has been carrying since 2001 – the same year he started fudging Satyam's accounts. As per medical reports, he is suffering from Hepatitis C infection, a condition that slowly destroys the patient's liver. Over the years, Raju has consulted even doctors in the US about this, but it has been of little help. Raju's health condition has been aggravated by the fact that he has plaque in two coronary arteries. His heart condition would require administration of cholesterol lowering drugs, but these might damage his already fragile liver. There seems to be no end to Raju's woes.

Index